Whatever Happened to

Fried Chicken?

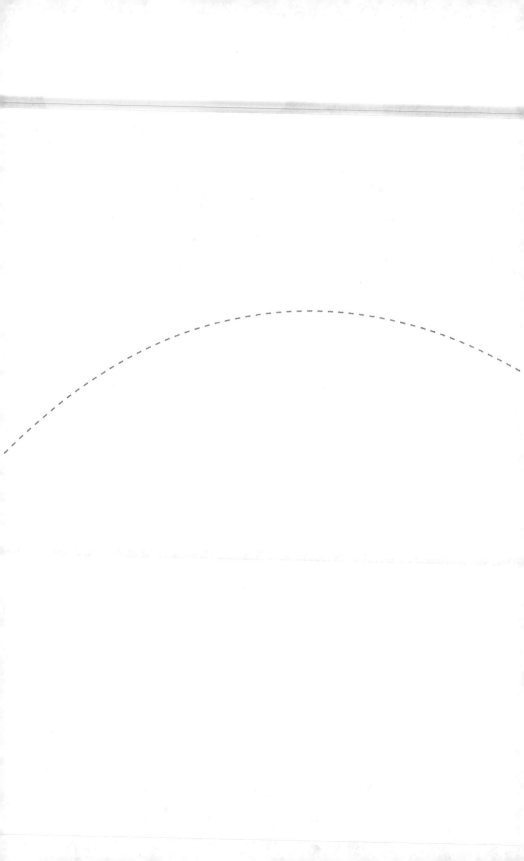

Whatever Happened to

Fried Chicken?

Is Old Time Religion Good Enough for Me?

Celine Sparks

Publishing Designs, Inc.
P. O. Box 3241
Huntsville, Alabama 35810

Cover illustration: Phyllis Alexander

Book design and layout: Crosslin Creative
Images: VectorStock, dreamstime, 123RF

"Old Time Religion" hymn design by Robert Jay Taylor, Taylor Publications LLC

Printed in the United States of America

Publisher's Cataloging-in-Publication Data

Sparks, Celine, 1964—
Whatever Happened to Fried Chicken / Celine Sparks.
Thirteen chapters.
1. Women—Christian living. 2. Traditional Values. 3. Humor.
I. Title.
ISBN 978-0-929540-87-0.
248.8

To Abram, who grew from a boy to a man during the
writing of this book. From toy trucks, stick swords
and paper soldiers. Whatever happened to that?

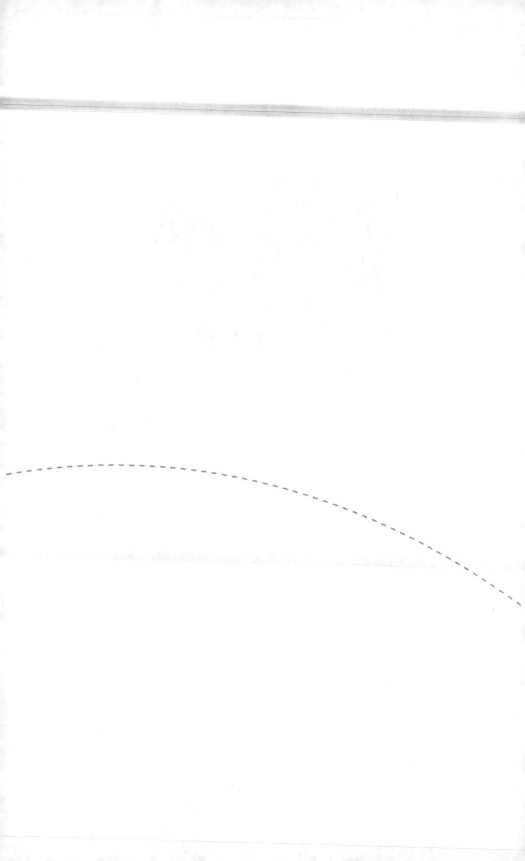

CONTENTS

INTRODUCTION

My dad eats a candle from his birthday cake every year. If it didn't happen, we would be a little uneasy. That's the way it is with traditions. We hold to them tight like a candle, never realizing that the wax is melting within our grip, and they're slowly and surely slipping away from us.

It raises the question, "Whatever *did* happen to fried chicken?"

Pretty soon a celebration is a memory, a centerpiece takes up attic space, and we find ourselves droning on about what used to be to a generation that looks up from their touchscreens long enough to say, "Huh?"

This book attempts to answer the spoken and unspoken "huhs" that pop up when we look back over our shoulder, sometimes with a "what in the world were we thinking?" and sometimes with a "why did we let that go?"

Don't worry, and don't feel like you must humor me as I bore you with things you're too young to remember or too old to . . . remember. This book is not so much a chronicling of the past as a challenge to the future. Let's bury what we mourn, and resurrect what we must. Let's laugh at what we did back then, and cry because we don't do it anymore.

I never really meant for the focus of this project to be a creek bank or a plate of fried chicken any more than Jesus meant for our concern to be for a camel trying to get through the needle.

Whatever happened to fried chicken? I'm not sure, but the piece I miss most is the backbone. In some areas, we've compromised until all we have left is the wishbone. We wish somehow we could restore the fervor without repeating the failures.

It's a good idea, and far more than just a wish. Join me as we borrow from the best of our past to get to the best of our future. And if we're going to go back in time in order to move forward, let's go way back. The problem with pulling our practices from the era of our mothers or our grandmothers is that we're a couple of thousand years off.

So we must reach past the anecdotes and pull with all our might for the antidote. When we examine, internalize, apply, and embrace God-breathed guidance and ground rules, we will get what we are seeking. Our equipment may be different from those of the filmstrip era or the paper-fan climate control, but nevertheless, we will be equipped (1 Timothy 3:16–17).

Between chapters, you will find sections titled *A Favorite Piece.* Skip over them if you like; they're not pertinent to salvation or spiritual sustenance. However, they might help a little with sanity. They are just there to prod a little laughter, a God-given blessing that we often get too busy to enjoy. God knew about endorphins before medical experts could spell them. It's why some of our most humorous memories are from campaign trails far from home, or from chilly hospital rooms in the middle of the night. God knew we would need a burst of laughter right about then in order to gear up for the next big thing.

I was actually in a hospital room when I first pondered the idea for this book. I tapped out a couple of lines as my daughter Miriam lay nearby with a ruptured appendix. It was a total shift in gears from the book underway at the time.

What I thought was an overnight stay turned into a week, and then into five additional days. Every time we turned a corner, we met a new obstacle. I prayed and it seemed the world prayed with me. Of course it wasn't the world, but the host of the redeemed.

She eventually had a temporary port put in, was treated with home health care, and on April 17, 2011, a full month after she was admitted to ER, was released from any further treatment. She was well. Hallelujah!

But during that time, *Whatever Happened to Fried Chicken?* began to take form. In cramped living quarters with very few spending quarters, memories rolled around in my mind and spilled out onto the keyboard. When I plunged into the scriptures for comfort for my mother worries, I came up for air with extras for the pages of this book.

This was written in pajama pants and fuzzy socks which would have probably been an outrage during the fried chicken era. But here it is: the product of hardcore prayer, hand wringing and nail biting; long days and restless nights; blessed assurance and peace that passes understanding. And oh yeah—a couple of rounds of laughter that we thought were going to rupture something beyond the appendix.

Those are the things I wish for you as you read: hardcore prayer, blessed assurance, peace, laughter, and when you need it most, fuzzy socks.

Celine

Whatever Happened to
Fried Chicken?

Bring Back the Hospitality

A blue willow platter full of crispy fried chicken sat dead center on the worn enamel topped table. Four boys, one girl, and three rules were also set down before the guest arrived.

First, be on your best behavior. "Behave" is a word moms have surely used since Eve and Jochebed; one that no kid knows the meaning of exactly, but everyone can pinpoint that it has something to do with not picking your nose and waiting until later to punch your brother.

Second, the guest goes first! Children weren't to touch a kernel of corn or the eye of a pea until the honoree, the visiting preacher, filled his plate.

Third, and most important, since the mother repeated it a half-dozen times to make sure every child understood, no one was to get seconds on chicken. It was all they had. There was only one piece per person, or as she said in those days, "a piece apiece."

This was long before I existed, but my mother Johnnia was the little girl at the table eyeing the chicken thigh, and as the platter was passed along that night, so was the following story forever after.

Johnnia cringed as she saw that preacher reach for the chicken thigh, but *c'est la vie*. The chicken did have two thighs after all. But then the unthinkable happened, at least in her young mind. The preacher's fork made another stab at the plate to get another piece—the drumstick, the leg—and while the boys just gasped under their breath, Johnnia blurted out in protest. "There's only a piece apiece. Right, Mother? There's only a piece apiece!"

My grandmother could have kicked her under the table, but all true mothers know that this produces one universal result: "Hey! What are you kicking me for?"

Those were the days when hospitality spoke but one language: fried chicken.

What happened? Even I can remember when fellowship meals were heavier on fried chicken than the graveyard is on concrete angels. Back in that day, if you got a helping of everything as you went down the long folding tables like we do now, you would have thirty-two chicken parts on your plate. Fried chicken was the official dish of good Christians everywhere.

We didn't even know how to spell *cholesterol* back then, but we were pretty sure it was an island down there somewhere. Now? Now we're a health conscious society. Now we count the fat grams instead of the pieces. And now the only person that's happy is the chicken.

But we'll make it. As hard as this may be to believe, nowhere in the scriptures is the term *fried chicken*. It's harder to accept than the price of

Even I can remember when fellowship meals were heavier on fried chicken than the graveyard is on concrete angels.

gasoline, but it may be that the day of fried chicken ruling the religious roost is gone, never to return. We'll just have to settle for broccoli casserole and taco soup. With great difficulty, I can succumb to that as long as the chicken didn't take other things with her when she rounded that corner—things more nurturing and sustaining, more valuable, and more attached to scriptural mandate. If she did, stop that chicken! Bring back the essentials.

> Continuing daily . . . from house to house, they ate their food with gladness and simplicity of heart (Acts 2:46).

Bring Back the Fellowship!

First of all, I'm afraid that chicken strutted off with the fellowship and together-time experienced in common meals. I remember years ago the radio blaring out a song about an all-day singing and dinner on the ground. I didn't know what it meant, but I assumed it had to do with those times my mother was so concerned with having enough that she had us march in with two or three bowls each. Inevitably, there would be a pile of macaroni and cheese or au gratin potatoes in the parking lot. Mark it down; it was whatever she spent the most time preparing. Regrettably, it was dinner on the ground.

We rarely hear the words "dinner on the ground" anymore, but that's okay too, as long as we're still having it together, be it inside and on tables.

In Acts 2 we find the disciples together daily, breaking bread from house to house, eating their food with simplicity and gladness. It's the same chapter we use as a precedent for baptism, but somehow it breaks down for some of us about verse 46.

Recently a church member was talking to my husband about the number of times Christian brothers and sisters had been coming together for meals within a short period of time. "You know, I just think you can do that too much!" he said.

I couldn't disagree more. Too much encouragement? Too much bonding? Too much blending the lives of those who will help sustain one another through the roughest of times ahead? Too much simplicity? Too much gladness? If anything, the recent meals had been short of the mark because, while frequent, they had still missed the Acts 2 "daily" example.

Bring Back the Hospitality!

The second thing I'm concerned the chicken may have walked out with is the abundant hospitality. Our mothers and grandmothers had a knack for something more than just frying chicken. It seemed when the plate was passed around, every piece communicated the concern the cook had for taking care of those who needed it. She and the chicken worked together in that. They supported a family whose breadwinner was laid off, they supported the widow with the three boys still at home, they supported the family that was having out-of-town houseguests, and they supported the mother with the new baby. There wasn't anything that a plate of fried chicken, and maybe an orange cake, couldn't at least help you through.

Preachers and Wishbones

More than anything, I remember that official bird helping feed the visiting preacher. In the late seventies and early eighties, Franklin Camp taught a class for preachers every Monday in the Birmingham area. Preachers came from Montgomery, Atlanta, Tuscaloosa, Anniston, and every small town in between to fill their cups with brother Camp's great insight into God's holy Word. But after they filled their cups, they went to fill their plates.

When I got off the school bus on Monday afternoons, I knew what to expect. Cars would be lined down my driveway and halfway up the street, and I no sooner set foot in the yard than I could hear the laughter and fellowship. The meal my mama had made was all gone but the wishbone. But somehow those preachers lingered over empty plates because no one wanted to be the first to leave. There was too much camaraderie there, too much encouragement, too much simplicity and gladness. Some of these preachers would return to challenging circumstances, but brother Camp's Bible lessons and Mama's fried chicken could get them through another week of it.

Preaching was something Mama could do well only to the four of us. She wasn't a Greek scholar, and she didn't personally baptize a single soul. But her fried chicken and fried okra and turnip greens and squash had a huge part in helping those who took the gospel to every creature. Hospitality always does.

Hospitality Is for the "Haves"

But hospitality is for the "haves" to help the "have nots," right? Are you a "have" or a "have not"? Our house held six people—eight when the grandparents moved in. We had one bathroom, the carpet needed replacing, and the sheetrock was parting ways in a couple of places, but Mama was a "have." To repeat, you don't have to have to be a "have." You don't have to have a fancy house or a fine linen tablecloth or even a perfectly ordered den to have the gift of hospitality.

Brother Hugo McCord told of one of the most hospitable moments he had experienced on the receiving end. He went to a small clapboard house where the host, a mining family with two boys, had prepared him dinner when he was the "visiting preacher" at a gospel meeting. The dinner consisted of a bowl of mashed potatoes mixed with a couple of wieners cut in small pieces, and the dinner party sat on nail kegs (McCord 8). This family consisted

Our mothers and grandmothers had a knack for something more than just frying chicken.

of "haves." They had a home, they had an opportunity, they had a table, and they had some potatoes. Most of all, they had two boys who needed a real life lesson in how to show hospitality. I bet they remember that lesson to this day.

My husband and I, along with our first baby son, used to stay in Finger, Tennessee, with a widow named Evil Tidwell when we needed housing for the Freed-Hardeman University lectureship each February. Her first name couldn't have been more opposite

An Extra Helping

If you ever want to remember what old-school hospitality tasted like, follow this recipe:

1 hen, washed and cut up (Or select the pieces you like at the supermarket. I use a tray of drumsticks.)

2 cups buttermilk mixed with 1 teaspoon salt and ½ teaspoon cayenne pepper

2 cups flour, mixed with one teaspoon pepper, 1 teaspoon salt, 1 teaspoon garlic powder, and ½ teaspoon paprika

3 cups oil

Heat the oil in the skillet on medium-high. Dip each chicken piece in the buttermilk; then coat with the flour mixture and drop in the hot oil. Fry 15 minutes, and then turn, and continue to fry for another 15 minutes.

Line an antique platter with paper towels, and transfer the chicken to the platter. After the grease is absorbed, you can remove the paper towels.

If you want to get close, but still pass your next physical, put 2 tablespoons oil in a baking dish, and preheat at 350 degrees. Mix 2 cups crushed corn flakes with one teaspoon garlic salt and ½ teaspoon pepper. Dip each piece in the buttermilk mixture (in above recipe), coat with the corn flake mixture, and place in baking dish. Bake for 50 minutes, uncovered, turning once.

from her sweet disposition. She had two sisters named Oval and Woodrow, which made me wonder just what her daddy had been farming along with his corn crop in those days.

Anyway, on those cold February nights we would sit up late with Mrs. Evil in a tiny room around a wood-burning stove in straight-back chairs, not one of them matching any of the others. But there were extra doses of laughter, and we rested our heads at night on pillows of peace. It was better than the Marriott. Mrs. Evil was a "have."

As we have opportunity, let us do good to all . . . (Galatians 6:10).

It's More about Your Heart than Your House

Don't wait until your wallpaper matches your carpet and you get that faucet handle replaced to show someone hospitality. If you have a dish, if you have a table, if you have a bag of potatoes, then you are a "have." Most of all, if you have a daughter or son who needs to learn about hospitality in vivid color, you are an especially rich "have." You are a "have" that will one day be a "have not." It's inevitable for all of us. It's an opportunity that's slipping away from us like butter off a hot ear of corn. Seize the moment!

I hate to say it because I stand convicted when I do, but when we try to make our house perfect to impress the company, it is ourselves we are serving and not others. Which one of us doesn't feel more comfortable in a home where we don't get whiplash from flinching every time our child brushes up against a piece of furniture or looks too closely at a knickknack?

Martha was distracted with much serving . . . (Luke 10:40).

One Thing Is Needful

Be sure you aim at your target. I think in Luke 10, Martha meant to be all about hospitality. She certainly was about much serving; she was about food and guests and hosting the first and greatest gospel preacher. But she was a little panicked about the situation, and when it didn't play out as she had pictured, stress started giving orders and hospitality jumped out the window from the bread pan.

In Christ's earthly lifetime of thirty-three years, do you know how many ordinary events did not make it into the scriptures? But God Almighty saw this little true story of a stressful kitchen episode as important enough to include for our learning. Why? Could it be that it's because He knows and loves us so well? He understood way ahead of time that two thousand years worth of those same episodes were looming for His daughters everywhere. His answer is the same today. "One thing is needful." True hospitality just doesn't stress out!

Reality Check

In John 12 we find Martha in the position of hospitality again, cooking and serving, but this time, not in a tizzy. What made the difference? Perhaps Jesus' rebuke, but Martha had also been through a sobering reality check since that last meal. She had lost Lazarus, and she had gotten him back. And there he was at the table. She could count her blessings in person, and she didn't have to count past one to know it was no longer important if the beans burned or the oil spilled.

Martha now knew more than anybody that hospitality is not about taking turns to go and see if my house is better than your house. Luke 14:12 gives us a heads up on that. Sometimes hospitality may be about buying a hamburger for the guy under the bridge. It may be about opening your home to a family that you don't even know but who came into town because a son or daughter or mother or father is in the nearby intensive care unit.

A When-It's-Convenient Thing?

"Do not forget to entertain strangers," Hebrews 13:2 says, and I don't think it's talking about song and dance or ventriloquism. The English Standard Version renders a better translation: "Do not neglect to show hospitality to strangers, for thereby some have entertained angels unawares." Most think this is a reference back to Genesis 18 when Abraham and Sarah were hospitable to three visitors who foretold Isaac's birth. We can't know for sure, but it certainly fits the bill. They were strangers, Abraham and Sarah were hospitable, and the visitors were messengers (angels).

Nice story, but pretty impractical for us, right? After all, Abraham lived life at a slower pace. We're juggling it like a circus act on an energy drink here. Don't kid yourself; life has always demanded more than we could give it. It has always been about making the choice to sacrifice something in order to squeeze something else in. Look at the language in this account:

> Abraham *hurried* into the tent to Sarah and said, "*Quickly*, make ready three measures of fine meal; knead it and make cakes." And Abraham *ran* to the herd, took a tender and good calf, gave it to a young man, and he *hastened* to prepare it (Genesis 18:6–7, emphases added).

He hurried, he ran, he said "quickly!" and the young man hastened!

Now exactly how is that different from our lifestyle? It sounds way too familiar to me. We're not commanded to be hospitable if we're not too busy. We're expected to be hospitable in spite of the fact that we're busy.

. . . seek to show hospitality (Romans 12:13 ESV).

A Safer Place and Time

Sometimes we simply are afraid to be hospitable to strangers. We tell ourselves that it's just not safe. It's not the same as it used to be in those simpler Genesis times. We live in a society filled with crime and evil. It seems we can't trust anyone.

Hmmm. Let's take a look at that hospitality episode again in chapter 18. Exactly in what kind of society did Abraham and Sarah live? They lived a few miles across the way from a city where you could not even find ten decent people if you were hard pressed. (And Abraham was very hard pressed.)

This was a society where people would come to your door and violently beat it down if you refused to be part of their rampant gang rape. It's just a little scary for me to read about, and Abraham and Sarah lived near it. While it's hard to exactly pinpoint where Sodom was—when God annihilates a city, even the dot on the map is gone—it's pretty well accepted that it was in the Dead Sea region. Even if it had been at the southernmost tip of the sea, it would have been only thirty miles from Mamre (Vos 275).

The events of the hospitality episode and the Sodom-and-Gomorrah episode didn't only take place in the same book of the Bible but the very same day. How far apart were the cities again? Well, it wasn't a strain for Abraham to see the smoke of the city by the next afternoon (Genesis 19:28).

Think we can be excused from hospitality because we live in a scary society? Try telling Abraham and Sarah that.

Err on the Doing Side

I'm not saying that we should start throwing caution to the wind, picking up hitch-hikers, and having our kids share a room with a street gang. But we need to have compassion for the displaced and act on that compassion as Abraham did. Some ways of being hospitable are safer than others, and we should seek those routes. However, sometimes we're going to find ourselves on the road from

Jerusalem to Jericho when we stumble across the beaten and help-less. As Christians, what are we going to do? Dodge by on the other side, or fully trust that God will be with us and walk right into the risk?

Can you ever really go wrong with hospitality? It's not a great feeling to know that you tried to show hospitality to someone, later to learn that person lied to you and used your kindness to support sin. However, keep this in mind. Over and over God condemns failure to help those who need it.

- Matthew 25:41–46—Then He will also say to those on the left hand, "Depart from Me, you cursed, into the everlasting fire prepared for the devil and his angels: for I was hungry and you gave Me no food . . ." "Lord, when did we see You hungry . . . and did not minister to You?" "Inasmuch as you did not do *it* to one of the least of these, you did not do *it* to Me." And these will go away into everlasting punishment, but the righteous into eternal life.

- James 2:15–16—If a brother or sister is naked and destitute of daily food, and one of you says to them, "Depart in peace, be warmed and filled," but you do not give them the things which are needed for the body, what does it profit?

- 1 John 3:17— But whoever has this world's goods, and sees his brother in need, and shuts up his heart from him, how does the love of God abide in him?

(See also Proverbs 28:27; 29:7; Daniel 4:27; Zechariah 7:10ff).

Not once in all of Scripture can I find Him condemning an act of helping someone who then fraudulently misuses that help. God doesn't hold us responsible for what the other guy chooses to do; he holds us responsible for what we choose to do. So if

We need to have compassion for the displaced and act on that compassion as Abraham did.

23

you err, do it on the side of hospitality. And by the way, if it's wrong to give blessings to those who misuse them, then God Himself is the chief offender.

A Birth or Death Situation

No, you really can't go wrong with hospitality, but for most of us it's a twice in a lifetime occasion. We dish it out in healthy helpings at the beginning of life and at the end. When a baby is born, we can't bring the casseroles fast enough. We somehow must think the mother is nursing twin cows instead of a six-pound infant. But even that windfall of food pales in comparison to that brought after the funeral. Mississippi songwriter Kate Campbell's *Funeral Food* nails it, "We sure eat good when somebody dies" (Campbell).

Usually between birth and death, there is this huge gap of time in which most people do the bulk of their living. It is in this space of time that we experience lean months, job losses, unexpected company, surgery, burnout, overtime, accidents, relationship crises, moving trucks—you name it! If it happens sometime between birth and death, it fits here. That fried chicken used to horn in on all of these occasions and bring a few of her friends. But when she left, she walked out with something precious.

. . . the words of the Lord Jesus, "It is more blessed to give than to receive" (Acts 20:35).

Creative Hospitality Traits

We've just stopped tending to one another's business, and that's not always a good thing. We've forgotten how to roll out care in a pie crust and serve strength from a skillet. But many of my spiritual mothers are still quite good at this. It seems to come as natural to them as a hole in your sock, but we need to understand that it probably isn't nature but years and years of intentional discipline and practice. We can learn from their creative hospitality traits. Here are a few of my favorites:

1. *Remember the widowers.* Most of them grew up in a generation where men did a lot of the work but very little of the cooking. They are most appreciative of a home-cooked dish, and it can go a long way in encouraging them.

2. *Multiply a blessing.* When you make homemade bread or cake, make it go further. Instead of encouraging one person, why not hit six or eight? Elderly couples, college students, widows, and caregivers cannot realistically eat a whole loaf of bread or cake, but one hefty slice can hit the spot, and it makes their day just a little sweeter to know someone was thinking of them.

3. *Take a breakfast.* Instead of the meals we usually think of, when someone is burning the candle at both ends already, it can be particularly tiresome to have to start her already jam-packed day in the kitchen. This is helpful for families with small children who are hit with an unexpected crisis, for caregivers who are adjusting to live-in parents, or just for helping church members who are hosting the visiting missionaries or guest speakers.

4. *Go simple with cheerful scents, sights, and flavors.* Young children love and need to be involved in caring. They can't cook a full-course meal, but they can pick flowers and put them in plastic bottles. They can put googly eyes on apples and oranges or wrap a ribbon around a candy bar or a pack of gum. What a day-changer this can be for a hall full of nursing home residents, and a life-changer for the impressionable little flower-picker.

5. *Check in online.* Use the social networks online to tend to other people's business in a good way. On any given day or night, you might find the following as a status. I found all of these in a few minutes.

- What a day!

- Today is my mommy's birthday and also her anniversary. Twenty-seven years. Just wish she and Daddy weren't so sick!

- Mom was released from the hospital to my sister's house. She will have to have someone with her 24/7 . . . and be very careful!

- Today was just X-rays (OW! Why do those things have to hurt so much?)

- Shelby's a brute . . . kid can pull a Christmas tree down on herself with one hand! Not bad for a 16-month-old, but not wonderful for Mom, who has put the tree together now three times . . .

Pick one, any one, and jumpstart hospitality again. But if you pick the "what a day!" person, you might want to ring the doorbell and leave a dish and a note on her doorstep. I don't think she has time for company today. And if you pick the person with the tree knocked over, you might want to carry paper plates.

Maybe you don't have time to kill the calf like Abraham did even if you hurry, but there's nothing wrong with picking up a pound of barbecue, a bag of fruit, or even a dozen doughnuts. (Well, there may be something wrong with that one if you don't share just one with me.)

The Short List

How many times have you heard that we can't earn our salvation? It's true; we're not capable. We can only respond to Christ's love in obedience. But while our works are inadequate to buy pardon, isn't it soothing to know that God values them, as measly as they may be? It's interesting what begins to stand out on our resume to God as we near and pass that three-score mark and possibility of widowhood:

Do not let a widow under sixty years old be taken into the number, and not unless she has been the wife of one man, well reported for good works: if she has brought up children, if she has lodged strangers, if she has washed the saints' feet, if she has relieved the afflicted, if she has diligently followed every good work (1 Timothy 5:9–10).

I can't help but notice that the things named in verse 10 line up heavily on the side of simple hospitality. I also notice that the lowliest act of all, washing the saints' feet, makes the short list. It takes me back to John 13. There they were, twelve friends with disgusting feet, and Jesus, Son of God, Prince of Peace, Lord of lords, and Savior of all became Washer of Feet. It is here, in the lowliest act of hospitality, and it is only here in all of Scripture that Jesus said, "I have given you an example, that you should do as I have done to you" (John 13:15).

So in God's list of important traits for the three-score lifetime, we have:

1. Bringing up children.
2. Lodging strangers.
3. Washing feet.
4. Relieving the afflicted.

If she has brought up children, if she has lodged strangers, if she has washed the saints' feet, if she has relieved the afflicted.
—1 Timothy 5:10

And I'll just imagine that if she were living today, she could fry up a mighty big skillet of chicken, too.

You might want to ring the doorbell and leave a dish and a note on her doorstep.

Soul Food

1. What other scriptures, besides Acts 2, reflect the idea that first-century Christians were doing a lot of eating together?

2. Is there ever a time when it is unsafe to help someone who needs it? How is it ever not worth the risk? What cautions can be put in place while still meeting the needs of those in crisis?

3. What act of hospitality has been done for you that stands out in your memory? What was going on at the time for you, and how did your life circumstances affect your appreciation of that act of kindness?

4. What events between birth and death that weren't mentioned in this chapter are good opportunities for us to horn in on someone's business with a little hospitality?

5. Go on facebook this week and find the status of a local friend that hints to you that this person could use a dish of encouragement. Bake it and take it, or if it works better for you, pick it up and take it.

6. Spend fifteen minutes and write down five statuses of that kind. Bring them to share with others; then put them on your fridge to remind you of the overlooked times when someone needs a little friendship and hospitality.

7. Consider a person you know who is like the woman in 1 Timothy 5:9. We often reflect on the Proverbs 31 woman, but this is her New Testament counterpart. Take a few minutes to honor that widow this week. You can split the dish from number 5 and take it to her or make a lunch date to a favorite place or invite

her to drop by for coffee and cake. If you're pressed for time this week, just bring the treat when you see her at church.

8. Feet washing is not so needed now as it was in New Testament times and locations, but what equivalent act of lowly, dirty, and necessary service can we do for others today?

9. John 13:15 is the only place Jesus used the word *example*. However, aren't there other instances when He portrayed lowly service? Name two, with Bible references.

A Favorite Piece

And speaking of the Marriott . . .

Oversized lush chairs await me beneath stained glass domes where beautiful people mingle. That's the way it looks on the commercial. We have a different experience up close.

We recently were privileged to secure a room in probably the most exorbitant hotel in Tennessee—one of those that has an entire forest in the middle of it with waterfalls and the Parthenon. We didn't even mean to go hiking, and thought that it was a speaking convention.

When we finally got past the jungle and into an actual hallway, we found there had been a mix-up, and we had a room with one bed instead of two. Since this was a luxury hotel with many amenities, we thought one of those might be to switch your room if it was the wrong one. In the words of Tweety Bird, we "tawt wrong." However, they would be glad to provide a rollaway bed, except . . . they didn't have any left. They do know there are six people in our family, right? And that two of our kids brought a friend?

Somehow, I found it quite humorous in the middle of the night that my husband and I were hanging on to the sides of a twin air mattress to keep from rolling off every time the other person moved, and we were paying three hundred dollars to do this. The only thing worse than trying to sleep in this arrangement is, as my husband let me know, trying to sleep with a person who is laughing hysterically and trying to take pictures.

Everyone else in our group had a grand time. They had balcony windows and were jumping on their beds. Don't attempt it with an air mattress. One of them came running up to us and said, "Guess what? They gave us the wrong room, and we have a huge living room, a kitchen, four beds, and a fold-out couch!"

At this same hotel, my husband decided the one amenity he would use was the safe. So he locked all the money he had left in it, along with a check that belonged to someone else. The money accommodations, I will say, worked much better than the people ones, and the money was so secure that no one bothered it the entire stay, including my husband who didn't even open the safe before checkout, and was halfway home before he made one sudden realization and fourteen phone calls.

Just between the sentences, "We will never do this again," and, "Next time we will sleep in the car," I reminded my husband that it was really much better than that time in Birmingham.

I looked at him over the top of an awkward stack supported by my belt and hip bone, and said, "I got this."

I arrived there a day ahead of him. It was supposed to be one of the grandest hotels in the city, but it was just about over for me when I first arrived, and a gigantic sewer rat, the kind that takes over cities in movies, ran across the portico. I had never seen one of these on the loose outside of a TV set, and I planned right then and there never to see one again if I could help it.

It was against my religion to pay fifteen dollars for parking, but after calling my husband, he told me to do it for safety reasons. My sister's husband, who also arrived the next day, had strong objections as well, so he ran out every two hours in his pajamas, walked two blocks, and put fifty cents in a parking meter.

After forking over fifteen dollars, I sure wasn't about to pay an additional fee for a bellhop, so I looked at him over the top of an awkward stack supported by my belt and hip bone, and said, "I got this." Then I dragged the rest of it and plopped it down next to an out-of-service elevator. I am not kidding. They never show this part on the commercial.

It's not that I minded going up the stairs, but I just couldn't get everything in one load, and I was afraid the head sewer rat was going to carry away the second load while I was gone with the first. Whereas other people have manageable luggage with sturdy shoulder straps and wheels, I had a hot pink plastic tub with a duct-tape secured lip. Providence kicked in when I spotted my neighbor who was at a chiropractor's convention in the same hotel, and he helped me up the stairs with my cargo.

Why does this stuff happen to me? Do upscale hotel operators meet once a year, randomly select a name, and unanimously decide to forever ban that person from having a four-star experience? If they have some kind of drawing, I won big!

In April of 2011, our power had been out for a week after tornadoes ripped through Alabama. My daughter's softball team had organized a trip to Nashville, and I had but one thought: a warm shower. I didn't care who won the ballgame. I didn't care if she got to be the starting catcher. I was consumed with the thought of a climate-controlled room with electric lamps and a hair dryer. I couldn't wish away the innings fast enough.

When I finally arrived at the hotel, here is what they had to say, "We don't have a reservation for you."

"But I made it ten days ago."

"Nope. Sorry. Nothing here."

"You're telling me I don't have a room?"

"There are no rooms. You see, tornadoes damaged much of Alabama and they have no power, and so we're completely full, and—"

"I know about it. Why is it that every single family on this softball team has a room—every single person but me?"

"Oh, here it is."

Huge sigh of relief.

"Yes, right here. Celine Sparks. It's for next Tuesday."

And those of us who have tried our luck on the website where they pick out a room for you at a surprise hotel, know to leave that alone. My friends Keith and Brenna got a cute little one with twin beds . . . on their honeymoon.

So just where *are* those oversized lush chairs? I may need to collapse on one when I see the fee for in-room bottled water.

CHAPTER 2

Whatever Happened to the Flash Cards?

Bring Back the Bible Knowledge

We had a stack of them this thick. They weren't colorful and they didn't have cartoon characters on them, but we knew them front and back, or at least we were supposed to. They were 5 x 8 index cards with a Bible question on the front and a matching answer on the back.

We drilled each other in Bible school, at the supper table, in the tree house, and sitting on the hood of the yellow Pontiac. It was a twentieth-century paraphrase of Deuteronomy 6:7, and it's why I know the ten plagues in order to this day. What happened to those cards?

I'm not allowed to forget that I was presented with an extremely difficult card once, namely "Who was Jacob's twin brother?" Even though I contorted my face in a number of ways and snapped my fingers repeatedly, which never seems to really help, but always buys you time, I could only come up with, "Aaaaah." So

33

my older siblings butted in to give subtle hints such as, "It rhymes with see-saw."

"Oh yeeeee-ahhhh!" my eureka came, "Beehaw!" I will never live it down should my birthdays surpass Methuselah's.

What happened to those cards? I recently found a stack of them bound together with a dry-rotted rubber band in the back of a dusty filing cabinet. I wanted to hug those relics close to my heart and could have shed a tear. It's a gone era. They have been replaced with full-color glossy workbooks, black lights, and video clips.

I applaud the new and brilliant. I'm among the first to welcome the innovative if it can open a child's heart and mind to absorb Bible knowledge. Let's use every avenue we can, but let's make sure all roads lead to the same destination as the old black-and-white 5 x 8s.

Bring back the Bible knowledge.

Get a Head Start

As the Lord's people, adults and children, our focus is on reaching out to the lost, and in turn reaching heaven together. But it's impossible to get there without knowledge of God's Word. The sooner we start, the better the journey. "Baby Einstein" videos promise parents that by starting early, their children will be high IQ frontrunners. We teach a child how to hold an aluminum bat just right before he knows first base from cheese crackers. How is it that we miss the fact that filling his head with Bible facts repeatedly is going to give him a better shot at heaven than tee-ball is ever going to give him at the MLB?

My people are destroyed for lack of knowledge (Hosea 4:6).

Is This Education?

But it's not just about the children. I've been amazed at some of the planned out—as in "on purpose"—adult Bible school curricula I have seen while visiting churches. I picked up a bulletin while at a wedding some time back, and one of the choices for Wednesday night Bible study was "flower arranging." What flowers? Mandrakes? Fig leaves? More recently, my son was practicing ball in a church fellowship area when I picked up another bulletin. This time the course was about farming, and the advantages of growing coffee. Other programs have revolved around lessons from viewing particular sit-coms. This may sound a little off the deep end, but just wondering if anyone else is thinking that in Bible class it might be a good idea to study, say, the Bible.

No wonder. No wonder this world seems to be just a little less psychotic than Lizzie Borden on laughing gas. No wonder no one seems to know right from wrong, or that there even is a wrong. No wonder *Jeopardy* contestants shy away from the Bible category as if it were an obvious case of the shingles. No wonder they can answer questions about cabinet members who died six hundred years ago to a country I've never heard of but have no idea who was thrown into a lion's den, even when given that it starts with a D and rhymes with *spaniel.* It really is exactly like God described Nineveh in Jonah 4:11. People simply do not know their right hand from their left. Why?

Zeal and Knowledge

There is some pretty exciting "church" going on. It resembles the concerts people camped out for when I was in high school. Many times it's housed in the movie theater before the first matinee on Sunday, and it's billed as a worship "experience." People

> Jeopardy contestants shy away from the Bible category as if it were an obvious case of the shingles.

> . . . They have a zeal for God, but not according to knowledge (Romans 10:2).

come out of there motivated—but for what? They have zeal, but is it according to knowledge?

Zeal is important and I would almost rather have zeal without knowledge than knowledge without zeal. But religious people are becoming less sure of what it is they're religious about. People simply do not know. They don't know that 1 Corinthians 6:9–10 gives a list of sins and then says that those who commit them cannot enter the kingdom of heaven. They don't know that they could make their lives far less miserable by practicing the revolutionary relationship principles of the Sermon on the Mount (Matthew 5–7). They are driving down a six-lane highway full throttle without a clue where they are headed, and with no road signs or markings.

Who's Clueless?

But what else can we expect? Hosea 4:6 warns us that people are destroyed for lack of knowledge. It's true. Being clueless about the Bible is wreaking havoc in our society. We see it in denominational assemblies from the traditional ones to those called "Cowboy Church." Admittedly, I'm not even sure what that means. We see it in our schools, in our governments, in the high-end mansions, and in the Section 8 apartments. But this verse in Hosea isn't talking about any of these situations. The first two words make that clear: "My people."

It wasn't about the heathen nations and their corrupt governments and sordid lifestyles. It was talking about His people Israel. They were the ones being destroyed for lack of knowledge. Is it possible that the same thing is happening to His people now? It's easy to shake our heads at those around us, but the warning is for His people.

But you are a chosen generation, a royal priesthood, a holy nation, His own special people, that you may proclaim the praises of Him who called you out of darkness into His marvelous light; who once were not a people but are now the people of God, who had not obtained mercy but now have obtained mercy (1 Peter 2:9–10).

The preceding quotation was written to Christians (1 Peter 5:14).

What You Don't Know Can Hurt You!

If Hosea 4:6 applies at all, it becomes scarier by the phrase as you read it. "Because you have rejected knowledge . . ." God says. Notice it is not a direct rejection of God. It is not a blatant disobedience of the "shalts" and "shalt nots." It's simply a rejection of knowledge. These guys just weren't picking up their Bibles enough—but they might have had some pretty awesome floral pieces. They simply did not know. Can God really hold us responsible for what we don't know? Read on.

Who Me? A Priest?

"I also will reject you from being priest for Me." What's that all about? The priests I know about wear black shirts with a little white square on the neck, and thus far, I have never done that. But those aren't the priests of the New Testament. We are! Take a second look at 1 Peter 2:9; it's in there.

An Extra Helping

Bring them back with a flair! Find free templates at bestteacherblog. com. Parents and Bible teachers can use the templates to drill facts, but these are not your mama's flashcards. Write your own Bible questions and plug them into the game show templates for *Jeopardy*, *Are You Smarter than a Fifth Grader?* *Who Wants to Be a Millionaire?* and others. Click the PowerPoint game templates link to get started.

In Hosea's time, the priests went to God for the people. They were the only ones who had a direct line to God, so they did the offering—the worshiping, the appeal for atonement—for the people. With the blood of Christ, He opened the door for all of us. We have all become priests—without white squares on our collars. We are a royal priesthood, as long as we keep that knowledge part.

Forgotten Children

If we reject knowledge, if we opt for flower arranging instead of scriptures, we are closing that direct line. A phone line that works only one way doesn't work at all. So how can we possibly maintain our position as priests if we have closed the direct line? This text in 1 Peter implicitly states that the royal priesthood is God's own special people. If we are rejected as priests because we ourselves reject knowledge, then we are concurrently rejected from being His people.

But it gets worse. "Because you have forgotten the law of your God, I also will forget your children" is the final verdict of Hosea 4:6. Sounds harsh; sounds unreasonable; sounds unloving. It is . . . on our part!

Which one of us would not lay our life on the line, if it meant saving one of our children? God receives no pleasure from the loss of any soul (2 Peter 3:9), but the spiritual guidance of our children rests heavily on our—the parents'—shoulders. God is communicating to us in the most alarming language the inevitable results of haphazard Bible study.

If we opt to engage in the "more urgent" or the "more interesting" or the "more popular" with our time while the Bible collects dust, it is certainly our prerogative, but be

It's not just a casual intake, but an agressive searching.

38

warned, be clear. The devastating consequences will not be restricted to our generation. Don't let it happen. If we do not teach our children, who will? And if we don't know, how can we teach? The verse doesn't point to a harsh God but to One who is considering the fate of our children more than those of us who are carelessly crowding out our only source of direction for their lives and eternal destiny.

Because you have rejected knowledge, I also will reject you . . . (Hosea 4:6).

The Main Thing

Don't read me wrong. I like flower arranging, and I can endure coffee if it's flavored like something else. I want you to know that I'm not being hypercritical, and it's way more than okay for Christians to get together in their buildings and learn an art that can be used in ministering to the bereaved or hurting, in a way that sometimes only flowers can. One lady's sweet-smelling ministry was criticized in Mark 14, and Jesus Himself said, "Let her alone" (v. 6). Neither would I criticize the use of a clip from a sit-com if it introduced a biblical study. Jesus did it all the time—I mean, except for the TV part.

Flower arranging—good. Bible study—better! It's okay to do a lot of good things but, to borrow a favorite cliché, the main thing is to keep the main thing the main thing.

Where's the "Daily"?

In our crazy lives, most elderships have had the wisdom to set aside a time during the week to pull us away from the world and into the Word. It's precious little. The New Testament precedent is daily, and not just a casual intake, but an aggressive "searching," an examination to see "whether these things were so" (Acts 17:11).

"Truth is fallen in the streets" was the sad condition of Isaiah's time (Isaiah 59:14). Has it happened on your street? Has it been laying there lifeless so long that some even question its existence? Can there even be an absolute truth? In John 17:17 Jesus said, "Sanctify them through thy truth; thy word is truth (KJV)." Jesus is not at odds with the Word of God. It's not an either/or situation. Jesus and the Holy Spirit are one with God the Father. The Holy Spirit, ultimate author of Scripture, cannot be more or less important than His godhead counterpart. Jesus relied on scripture, memorization, to defend Himself against Satan every time (Luke 4). Can we get by with less?

Bring back the flash cards.

> *. . . They received the word with all readiness,*
> *and searched the Scriptures daily . . .*
> —Acts 17:11

Soul Food

1. What childhood memory do you have of learning something through a rote memorization technique? Do you think you'll ever forget it?

2. A couple of examples were noted of what was being studied in churches rather than the Bible. On the flipside, what encouraging or interesting specific textual studies have you observed when you've visited other congregations? How can you incorporate these ideas into your personal Bible study or group studies with friends?

3. As teachers of children, how can we borrow the strengths of the old flash cards while incorporating the new and innovative to keep our children full of both zeal and knowledge?

4. What esteem does our society give to Bible knowledge? For one week, keep up with any reference to the Bible or Christianity by the media that you come across. Observe whether each was positive or negative.

5. Find a flyer for an event of a religious organization near you. Notice the drawing card that is advertised for the event. Does it support a trend toward or away from scriptural studies?

6. Take a look at the practices of the Old Testament priests. How do they parallel our service and relationship to God and others as Christians today?

A Favorite Piece

And speaking of aluminum bats . . .

We used to get by all summer without even one. That meant running over to Merita's every morning for three months and doing cannonballs into the horse trough. Mid-day we would sit on the hood of the pickup and play a few rounds of "What do you want to do?" "I don't know; what do you want to do?" We rode down steep inclines on bicycles with flat tires with another kid on the handlebars and no helmets, and lived to tell about it. My sister once raced us on the Big Wheel. That's the day we learned the Big Wheel doesn't come with brakes installed, as we watched her cruise across the highway at the end of the hill, trying to break her speed with bare feet on the pavement. She won!

We had reality back then. We were a match for any primetime show. We knew the biggest loser was the one who didn't see the poison ivy as he swung from the vine yelling "Geronimo" before we knew the correct term was "Cowabunga." The real housewives were the ones we didn't answer until they called our middle names, and the reason the race was amazing was because it was against a Doberman we didn't see until we had already hit his doghouse with a rock. We didn't need two nice judges and one sinister one to tell us Sandra Benefield was way off key as we rocked the tree house to the Bay City Rollers. We were survivors.

But we were not organized. We lived before parents got involved in summer fun. Oh, we played ball, all right, but we tagged up on Mimosa trunks and dared each other to run while we threw the ball up in the air. You could try it if you pushed your luck, and most of us did, but you would probably have a bruise on your back the exact size of a softball which, for the record, is not very soft.

Sometime between those days and these, a committee somewhere decided that juvenile delinquency, self-esteem issues, and how in the world to pay for the new statue on the square could all be solved with one catastrophic concept: organized ball. Whoever first termed it that has obviously never been to an actual game, in which nothing could possibly be more disorganized. The idea is to pay seventy-five dollars up front (per kid), and then watch a season of something slightly less organized than a group of deacons moving the contents of an eight-room house, which is another book.

The first lingo to be learned is the phrase, "Watch the ball!" They say this over and over to the six-year-old as if there are a whole lot of other options from his vantage point. The kid is looking straight ahead at what seems to be the ball, and I'm wondering at this point if some of the parents' mouths may be stuck in watch-the-ball mode, and if it would help them if I gave them

After the registration fee and parking, I could barely scrape up 29 cents for my share of the Slurpee.

a little slap like I do the CD player. The coach has a slightly extended vocabulary including "Good eye, good eye" and "Get down." I can see where the whole self-esteem thing is going since the child is constantly being affirmed because his eye is good.

Our family hardly says anything related to the actual sport, unless you count "Pass the Slurpee." This is our eleventh year in little league, so we're just a little proud that we know the ropes enough to bring our own lawn chairs, even though we haven't yet figured out how to get them back in the bag when it's over.

I still remember that first game when, in addition to "Watch the ball," we also yelled, "No, don't pick up the ball. Run! No, not that way, to the base, not the mound. Not that base, the other base, not that one either, no that—put down the bat! No, don't throw it!"

Some of the parents think their kids are actually playing lousy on purpose, I guess. They offer them a raise if they'll actually hit the ball, or catch the ball, or quit picking their nose. I've seen parents up the stakes to 40 dollars for a theoretical caught pop fly, still with no results. I'm wondering what kind of drugs these people must be peddling to afford that kind of bribe, being that after the registration fee and parking, I could barely scrape up 29 cents for my share of the Slurpee.

Nick's bat cost 219 dollars, Eric's, 249, but our son Abram's washed down the creek. It had no letters on it, black electrical tape for a grip, and looked like it had survived the Korean War. No matter how much their parents tried to pay their sons to use the high-dollar bats with metallic graphics of cobras chewing up baseballs, and autographed by some famous baseball player like probably Chuck Norris, they used what has been forever christened *Creek Bat*. I heard one parent say, "If you'll use the bat I bought you, I'll let you jump on the bed tonight for 10 minutes." It soon went up to 40 with no taker.

The deal was, *Creek Bat* would take a good batter around the bases twice, and the parents hated that with 249 dollars worth of pure hatred.

There have been benefits to the summer takeover. Our prayer life has been strengthened, praying fervently for rain and early elimination. We have learned to multi-task, watching children playing on several fields at the same time, pretending to know what was going on, and escorting grandparents from one fence to another, just in time to say, "Never mind. She just struck out. Turn around."

So as summer nears, I'm compelled to remember the words of that famous song, "Take Me Out to the Ballgame," and to wonder, *What park were they going to? Does anyone even sell peanuts and Cracker Jacks? Has any parent ever once said, "I don't care if I never get back"?*

I doubt it seriously, but if one ever did, I think the board member who made out the Saturday schedule was listening.

Whatever Happened to the
Tent Meeting?

Bring Back the Time Investment

I don't remember many of them myself. Where tents conjure in my mind muddy sleepovers with marshmallows and ghost stories, these were a tent of a different stripe. They had no sides, but were a huge worn and heavy canopy on intimidated rusty poles, and regrettably, there were no marshmallows.

I've stopped by at a handful of them in my lifetime on crooked back roads. We tried to revive the idea in the swamplands of Mississippi in the mid-nineties. It was a pretty successful run—but that's just it—it was a run; the tent thrown up one day, and a memory three days later.

Not so for the authentic tent meetings back in the day. I guess if you put that much back-work into erecting a town eyesore, you plan to leave it there awhile. So summers were spent gardening or roofing or working at the mill every day and going to tent meetings every night. No one nervously glanced at his watch as the long-winded preacher rang out the message.

No one feared she would miss a segment of a reality show or an inning of a ballgame. They were there for the long haul, and the ticking of the clock was upstaged by the wave of funeral home fans easing the sweat beads making trails down dust-coated faces.

No, I never really experienced those summers, but I do remember the part about attending one gospel meeting or another practically every single night from April through October. They were kind of like mosquitoes; there were plenty of them around. It was a common practice for meetings to last from Saturday to Saturday.

> Paul . . . continued his message until midnight (Acts 20:7).

Condensed Version

No one noticed much when some of them started on Sunday and ended on Friday.

But then the unthinkable happened, and I will never forget it. One of the nearby congregations ended its gospel meeting, not on a Friday, but on a Thursday night. We weren't sure if that could really be true or not, but the more we asked around, the more the rumor was confirmed.

We weren't convinced at first that this was scriptural, but the church got away with it, and soon many other congregations followed suit. It wasn't long before the Sunday-through-Thursday gospel meeting evolved into the Sunday-through-Wednesday one. Then we began to hear of weekend meetings, until finally we had the one-day gospel meeting.

I have to grieve the loss of the week-long meetings because they hold not only sentimental memories for me but the very spore of germination in the conversion of thousands; among whom are some of our pillars in the church today. In the parable of the sower, this was the good ground.

But while I grieve its passing, I'm in no way minimizing the effectiveness of the shorter efforts as they impact our current culture. If people will turn out for the gospel message on top of a water tower on alternate Thursdays at 3:00 A.M., then I believe that's the method we should use. We should use what is effective in reaching people, and sadly, that is probably no longer the tent meeting.

Bring Back the Time Investment

While we can't bring back the tent meeting, we can bring back the time investment. If we are opting for shorter sermons in meetings of less duration, it had better be because we are trying to do more and not less. Instead of walking into a tent every night of the summer, are our days and nights still packed with evangelistic campaigns, Bible camps, marriage strengtheners, vacation Bible schools, community outreach days, one-on-one studies, and every good work that presents itself?

Interesting phrase—*every good work.* It's not that we add up the number of summer, or any other season, activities and see if we can make a passing grade or a score higher than our neighbor's. No score is high enough to merit good standing with God (Luke 17:10), so are we really to attempt to be involved in every good work? Let's take a look.

- And God is able to make all grace abound toward you, that you, always having all sufficiency in all things, may have an abundance for every good work (2 Corinthians 9:8).

- That you may walk worthy of the Lord, fully pleasing Him, being fruitful in every good work (Colossians 1:10).

The ticking of the clock was upstaged by the wave of funeral home fans.

47

- Now may our Lord Jesus Christ Himself, and our God and Father, who has loved us and given us everlasting consolation and good hope by grace, comfort your hearts and establish you in every good word and work (2 Thessalonians 2:16–17).

- Well reported for good works: if she has brought up children, if she has lodged strangers, if she has washed the saints' feet, if she has relieved the afflicted, if she has diligently followed every good work (1 Timothy 5:10).

- Therefore if anyone cleanses himself from the latter, he will be a vessel for honor, sanctified and useful for the Master, prepared for every good work (2 Timothy 2:21).

- Remind them to be subject to rulers and authorities, to obey, to be ready for every good work (Titus 3:1).

- Now may the God of peace . . . make you complete in every good work to do His will (Hebrews 13:20–21).

So the question was, "Are we supposed to enlist in every good work?" Inspired scripture answers with a resounding "Yes!" But from the pool where we are in over our head and treading the waters of social standing, career ladders, futile competitions and new carpet, we strain, *Are you sure?*

Real Life

We can sing some pretty four-part harmony from the pews, but I'm wondering if we should alter the words just a little to reflect what's really going on. Sometimes if we were more honest, we would sing:

I Surrender Some.

Sweet Seconds of Prayer.

Less, Less about Jesus.

Each Year I'll Do a Golden Deed.

We'll Work 'til Jesus Comes—Or at Least 'til Football Season Starts.

Let Me Live Close to Thee Sundays from Nine to Ten.

Tell Me the Story of Jesus, but Hurry.

Are Your Garments Mostly Spotless? Are They Whitish?

And we would list our favorite hymn as *Lord, Dismiss Us.*

I saw, with my own eyes, a church marquee which read—and I quote verbatim: *"Dress Casual. Short Sermon. Eat Early."* What a contrast to the song we used to hear blaring from the gospel radio station about an all day singin', and dinner on the ground! Oh, both

An Extra Helping

Here are two ways to be involved in "every" good work, even when your feet can't get you there.

1. *Elisha Basket:* Keep an Elisha basket stocked in your vacant bedroom, and let all local congregations know the room is ready for every good work. The basket serves as a hostess when you are committed elsewhere, and contains: Pen, paper, snacks, magazine, TV remote (if applicable), towel, washcloth, toiletries, a house key, and directions to breakfast foods in the pantry.

2. *Lydia Tin:* Keep a calendar of all your congregation's events, and provide cookies (recipe below) for those outside your involvement zone (i.e., teens, singles). Add ongoing personal studies that you know of on a calendar, too, and send cookies to those. Ask for the Lydia tin back for a refill.

Easiest Homemade Cookies Ever

1 cake mix (any flavor)
½ cup self-rising flour
⅔ cup oil
2 eggs

Combine and bake at 350 degrees on ungreased pan for 10 minutes.

ideas had the same ending, but the new way determines to get there faster than the old.

Wait Here; I'm Busy Opening Presents

It's as if we view God as a pestering salesman, and we politely say, "God, I'd love to, but I don't have the time." What thing is it that you'd like to do for the Lord if you weren't so busy? What good work of the church would you like to be involved in if you only had the time? And what part of church have you found yourself missing, because it got crowded out of your hectic schedule? Now step back and look at the picture. What activity is it that you're doing that's replacing what you'd love to do for the Lord? I dare you to think of one that's not a blessing that He himself gave you. (I'm not talking about sickness; if you're taking care of the sick, that *is* your good work.)

- *Are you neck high in your children's sports activities?* Who gave you those children? Who was it that you pled with through nine months of pregnancy that they would be healthy, and now they're healthy enough to run the length of a soccer field more times than you can count without a calculator?

- *Are you working on a particularly demanding project or course?* Who gave you that ability? Who's really providing the salary or the tuition, even if it's "borrowed"?

- *Is there just too much work on the house, the lawn, that absolutely must be done before you get involved in teaching another soul or feeding a hungry mouth?* Whose house? Whose lawn?

Two verses come to mind: "Also that every man should eat and drink and enjoy the good of all his labor—it is the gift of God" (Ecclesiastes 3:13), and "Every good gift and every perfect gift is from above, and comes down from the Father of lights, with whom there is no variation or shadow of turning" (James 1:17). It's as if the Father is calling our names, and we can't answer right now because we're too busy opening presents.

Bigger, Not Better

The tent has folded for more luxurious accommodations. We have climate-controlled cathedral-looking structures that we drive to, riding on leather seats to the tune of a-whole-lot-of-money per gallon, instead of walking there down a gravel road. The crowds are still large as long as the promise is upheld: "Dress casual. Short sermon. Eat early."

We ought to be ashamed.

Soul Food

1. Ask an older member of the church to recount what the gospel meetings were like in her earliest memories? How did they differ from the ones we have today? How are they the same?

2. In your opinion, what happened to the practice of going to church practically every night of summer? How would that work today in our culture?

3. What are the advantages of having shorter evangelistic efforts? What are the disadvantages?

4. Brainstorm with other ladies to come up with an effective "one-day good work." With the permission of your leadership, get creative, enthusiastic, and organized to make it happen. While it is only one day, it is one more day in addition to those good works already being done—a great time investment for His kingdom.

5. Read Ephesians 2:1–10. This passage alludes to three entities and their working, works, or workmanship. Who are they?

6. Also in this same passage, find the beautiful attributes of God which ensure our salvation. There are several. How do these, at the same time, both negate and necessitate our good works?

7. How does 2 Thessalonians 2:16–17 motivate us to invest more time in spiritual things?

A Favorite Piece

And speaking of tents . . .

How is it that we pay money to suffer? I refer not just to the opera and the corn dog but also to one of our great American pest times—camping! It really does sound like a good idea, in theory. On commercials kids sit around a campfire in plaid flannel shirts eating s'mores and smiling at their parents. That's because it's a commercial in which people are paid to look like they're having a good time, and which does not show the footage of how many times the campfire went out before the smiled-upon father siphoned gasoline out of the car and onto the sticks.

It is also not raining. Nor has it rained for the past five days straight, so that the tent now looks like Mount St. Helens had a baby.

But let's back up. I want to discuss this whole tent design thing, which was obviously done by Picasso, being that there are countless randomly shaped items, all of which, when they come together, mean absolutely nothing. The price tag also reflects obvious museum rarity.

So here's how it works. The first idea is to sell the tent in a bag which securely holds all the contents once. After that, there is no possible way to get those same items back in the bag, even after ripping it four times. The contents consist of numerous plastic poles which ingeniously expand and lock into place while pinching your fingers. So a second ago, you were walking around the campground with a little stick, and now you're hopping around all over the place with an eleven-foot pole, shaking your other hand and pronouncing things which sound an awful lot like Pokémon's top twelve battlers. We suddenly know why they termed this part of the campground "primitive."

But the deal is, as the night grows dark, you have about a dozen of these awkward poles, and pretty much a nylon blob on the ground is supposed to hold them all. Everyone under twelve from miles around is eager to help. Everyone over age twelve from miles around is staring out at you from an air-conditioned RV during commercials and posting YouTube videos of you all over the world which are generating billions of comments, all of which end with LOL.

After 132 minutes of this kind of fun, sliding poles in and out of casing way too short for them, and getting hung on the casing every time, you throw the directions in the river and do it your own way. What you end up with looks like the state of Alaska with parachute pants hanging down to one side. The tent construction is over, and you suddenly have elevated respect for the apostle Paul.

One more tip: The poles break when either the wind blows or your tent becomes base in the game of campground hide and seek.

So on to more fun activities, right? The main one being eating. Since there is no fire for the s'mores or the hot dogs due to the current flood levels, we eat handfuls of Rice Krispies, Vienna sausage from the can, and cookies which didn't have chocolate chips when we arrived, but do now.

And then on to the tent to snuggle in the sleeping bags and listen to the sound of crickets as we drift off to sleep, singing favorite campfire songs and telling ghost stories. We do a varied version of that. It's where we bring all the sand and dirt in on our shoes that we possibly can, and then discover that we have staked our tent down on top of the central root sustaining a tree that must be a national monument. We have purchased a three-room-tent to find that everyone wants to sleep in the same room, and ultimately my husband decides to go out and sleep in the cooler.

It is here that my children become so enamored with the camping equipment that you would think they had never seen a flashlight in their life. There seems to be a constant race to see exactly who can get in Guinness first for operating the on/off switch the most number of times. (I'm pretty sure the four-year-old won.) They drain fourteen dollars worth of batteries just before someone actually needs the flashlight for a valid reason, such as to light the long path to the bathroom. And I check once again just to make sure: We're paying to do this, right?

This seems to be quite an emergency need, so we run uphill sloshing through the mud without flashlights. My daughter runs ahead, and when she flies through the wood slat door, I hear a piercing shriek that lets me know surely Charles Manson has escaped from prison.

In reality, it was Miriam's reaction to the fact that every known specie of insect—and I think a few unknown—were attracted to the one source of light in the forest: the bathhouse.

It's not that I didn't enjoy the whole outdoor experience, but next time we're going to invest in pain and suffering, do you think we could just skip the tent-thing and go straight to the ER?

Whatever Happened to
The Creek?

Bring Back the Urgency of Baptism

I think it would be simpler to bring back the creek. You wouldn't have to worry if the heater in it was on or off, and subsequently you wouldn't have to call the deacon over building and grounds after he had gone to bed, and drag him out in his pajamas. You would never be surprised to get to the creek and find out, *Man, it's empty again!* You would never succumb to singing all four stanzas of nearly every song in the book while it was being filled up with a water hose. No one would have to drop by once a week with a gallon of bleach and scrub the side of the bank. You wouldn't have to get a dozen estimates for how much a crack in the bottom of the creek is going to set us back. Best of all, you would never have to wonder if a candidate for baptism was going to fit in that thing or not. The creek would hold them; it was one size fits all.

The Jolene Hop

Not so with the baptistery. My husband could vouch for that, as
could practically any preacher since the invention of fiberglass.
Each one has a story; we have several. My favorite is Jolene's. Jolene
weighed quite a bit more than my husband, which was not hard to
do in those days. He quietly explained to her that she was to bend
her knees, and that would make the process of going under and
coming back up much easier for both of them. She nodded that she
understood, but I guess her knees didn't. When the appropriate time
came, the inappropriate thing happened. Instead of bending and
going under as my husband's arm kind of forced her down, she
hopped backward. Weightless in the water and attached at the arm,
my husband took the hop with her. They tried again. Same result.
This kept going on for a while until it was more entertaining, and
they were better partners than any of the star competitors on the
TV show. Oh, and yes, it was a Sunday morning baptism, and not
one of those middle-of-the-week things where only a few people are
around. He finally got her under, and the reality of what had happened, the blood of Jesus Christ had cleansed her from all sins, far
overshadowed anything which had happened in the previous long
minutes. I wish I could say it turned out as good for my husband's
pants. The waders are a good idea in theory, but though they are
designed to keep water out, they often achieve the opposite, bailing
water in, particularly if your best suit has just been dry cleaned.

See, here is water. What hinders me
from being baptized? (Acts 8:36).

Landmark of Cleansing

Yeah, the creek would have come in handy that day. With no
walls to worry about crashing into, and with the looming danger

of landing on a sharp rock every time she hopped, I think Jolene would have gone under without a production. The creek holds special memories for a dwindling generation. Oh, there is nothing significant in it or its water. After all, it is Christ's blood alone that cleanses, but the creek serves as a meaningful landmark. Driving the crooked mountain roads of North Carolina, my friend Radnor Curd used to say without fail when we passed a certain creek, "See that? All my sins are flowing down that water right there." I would answer, "Man, I hope I never have to get in that creek."

But the reality is, I sure am glad that so many people have got in the creek—and the baptisteries, and the camp swimming pools, and the hospital bathtubs. It's urgent; it's paramount. But there are a lot of people who will tell you it isn't. Don't believe them.

Take a Number

Baptism is urgent, not because it was when the traveling preachers escorted crowds of people to the creek, not because it was for your grandmother or for mine or for Radnor Curd, but because it was from the beginning of the existence of the Lord's church. If the Bible teaches that baptism is anything at all, it teaches that it is urgent.

Let's just look at the examples we have of baptism from the book of Acts:

- *Then those who gladly received his word were baptized; and that day about three thousand souls were added to them* (Acts 2:41).

- *But when they believed Philip as he preached the things concerning the kingdom of God and the name of Jesus Christ, both men and women were baptized* (Acts 8:12).

- *Now as they went down the road, they came to some water. And the eunuch said, "See, here is water. What hinders me from*

She nodded that she understood, but I guess her knees didn't.

being baptized?" . . . So he commanded the chariot to stand still. And both Philip and the eunuch went down into the water, and he baptized him (Acts 8:36–38).

- *Immediately there fell from his eyes something like scales, and he received his sight at once; and he arose and was baptized. So when he had received food, he was strengthened. Then Saul spent some days with the disciples at Damascus* (Acts 9:18–19).

An Extra Helping

When you learn of someone's baptism, use the following directions to make them a bookmark:

Adjust the margins on your computer, so that you can print the following to be 1½ to 2 inches wide by about 5 inches long.

After printing and cutting, lay on a 2 x 9 inch lightweight fabric strip such as paisley, calico or dots, so that the fabric makes a nice border on just the top and bottom edge. (Fabric trimmed with pinking shears is best.) Laminate, and give it to your new sister to serve as a lifelong reminder of the paramount importance of what took place.

* In the case of a new brother, adapt the text, add other names (i.e. husband, children, sisters) to your signature, and use solids or sport-themed fabric.

Never forget that on this day:

Date _____

Your sins were annihilated, your place was claimed in heaven, your life course was charted, you entered into Christ where all spiritual blessings exist, you became the devil's militant opponent and beloved heir of God your Father, and you became my sister.
I love you in Christ,

_____
Signature*

- *So I sent to you immediately, and you have done well to come. Now therefore, we are all present before God, to hear all the things commanded you by God . . . And he commanded them to be baptized in the name of the Lord. Then they asked him to stay a few days* (Acts 10:33–48).

- *And on the Sabbath day we went out of the city to the riverside, where prayer was customarily made; and we sat down and spoke to the women who met there. Now a certain woman named Lydia heard us. She was a seller of purple from the city of Thyatira, who worshiped God. The Lord opened her heart to heed the things spoken by Paul. And when she and her household were baptized, she begged us, saying, "If you have judged me to be faithful to the Lord, come to my house and stay." So she persuaded us* (Acts 16:13–15).

- *And he took them the same hour of the night and washed their stripes. And immediately he and all his family were baptized. Now when he had brought them into his house, he set food before them; and he rejoiced, having believed in God with all his household* (Acts 16:33–34).

- *And he departed from there and entered the house of a certain man named Justus, one who worshiped God, whose house was next door to the synagogue. Then Crispus, the ruler of the synagogue, believed on the Lord with all his household. And many of the Corinthians, hearing, believed and were baptized. Now the Lord spoke to Paul in the night by a vision, "Do not be afraid, but speak, and do not keep silent"* (Acts 18:7–9).

- *When they heard this, they were baptized in the name of the Lord Jesus* (Acts 19:5).

- *And now why are you waiting? Arise and be baptized, and wash away your sins, calling on the name of the Lord* (Acts 22:16).

> And now why are you waiting? Arise and be baptized . . .
>
> —Acts 22:16

Pull Over!

There seems to be a recurring theme of immediacy here, one that we're missing most often today. From those first three thousand on the day of Pentecost, there is never a single example in the entire Acts history of the church where those who believed were not baptized on the very same day. Why? Why, out of three thousand people, wasn't there someone who wanted to go home and think about it overnight? Why didn't just one person want to wait until her aunt was in town so she could see it? Because it was paramount. It was essential to being forgiven (Acts 2:38), to being saved (Mark 16:16), and to being in Christ (Romans 6:3). What was broken needed to be fixed, and there is urgency in that. It's why we have ER's open all night.

When Mattianne was four, she was retelling her Bible class story of Phillip and the Ethiopian eunuch in Acts 8, and she grossly paraphrased by saying, "Stop the car! I want to be baptized." It might be a paraphrase, but it's exactly what happened. They spotted the water in the middle of their study and their journey, commanded the chariot to stand still, and both of them got in the water. Why? Why didn't the eunuch reason that when he got back home and things settled down a bit, this would be one of his first priorities? It was too urgent. It obviously couldn't wait.

Late for Supper! (Acts 9:18–19)

In Acts 9 Saul had experienced quite an ordeal for the past few days, and had not only been blind, but verse 19 implies he was weak. But when he learned the truth, and when the scales fell from his eyes, there was something yet to be done before he could eat and receive strength, and of course that thing was his own baptism. Why? Why was it more important than physical nourishment at a time when he was so weak?

If One More Thing Happens Tonight . . . (Acts 16:33–34)

But the jailer's conversion in Acts 16 is by far the strongest defense for the urgency of baptism. Let's take a look at these last twenty-four hours. Paul and Silas, because of a good work they had done, had been taken to officers, a mob had clouded the issue further, the two were beaten extensively and were not only put in prison but immobilized with the uncomfortable stocks of that time. That's just the prelude. There was an earthquake—a big one!—and a subsequent attempted suicide. The events of the night were tremendously overwhelming.

If baptism were an optional outward religious ceremony, any person with a fraction of a degree of rational behavior would have opted for prayer, sleep, clear thinking, emotional recovery from the events, and needed nourishment. But that is not what happened. Notice the wording:

> And he took them the same hour of the night and washed their stripes. And immediately he and all his family were baptized (Acts 16:33).

Afterward, there was a meal and rejoicing, and apparently a return to jail, but not until the crucial event took place (Acts 16:34–35).

Why are you waiting? Arise and be baptized, and wash away your sins (Acts 22:16).

No Hesitation (Acts 22:16)

There is only one reason for such extreme measures, and that is that baptism is absolutely essential to put one into a right relationship with God, and in the midst of the events of that night, the jailer wanted his life right with God and his soul prepared for judgment.

In Acts 22 Paul remembers the words of Ananias to him, words which followed so close on the heels of the previous message that one wonders just how much waiting could have been involved. But isn't hesitation determined by the urgency of the situation? We find ourselves yelling at the base runner on the little league field, "Why did you hesitate?" This is said to a child who has never quit running, but merely slowed his stride for part of a second! We're communicating what Ananias did, "Why are you waiting?" Only the rest of Ananias's plea is about an outcome more important than a baseball scoreboard. "Arise and be baptized, and wash away your sins."

I guess that explains it. Those of us who have the sin problem also have a solution. What are we waiting for? Wash it away! So why? Why are so many people waiting? Baptism gets us into Christ (Galatians 3:27), saves us (1 Peter 3:21), and forgives us (Acts 2:38).

But is it possible we overemphasize its importance? Some say so. But if we do, we stand in good company. Jesus Christ, Lord of lords, whose personal blood is in the process, had this to say, "He who believes and is baptized will be saved" (Mark 16:16). Could any simple truth be more conclusive?

Reasonable Deception

How is it that most of the religious world trips up on it? I believe it is Satan's favorite tactic. "He is a liar and the father of it" (John 8:44). He is not interested in lying to us about minimal details, but he cunningly goes for the kill. He wasn't interested in talking to Eve about the other trees in the garden, but quickly moved to the one that would deliver death. He was deceptive and somehow made it sound reasonable and good. He's still the same guy. He goes straight for the very implement that will take away the one thing he needs us to hang on to—sin. And somehow he makes it sound reasonable and good that we can take care of it some other way. Sorry liar! Don't bite his apple.

Get to the creek, and not a minute too soon.

. . . and he went on his way rejoicing.
—Acts 8:39

1. What circumstances, if any, warrant waiting before a person puts on Christ in baptism?

2. Which is your favorite baptism event from the book of Acts? What makes it stand out to you as the best?

3. Research how baptisms are being conducted in different parts of the world. How does the expedient differ while the purpose stays the same? If you are in a group study, let each person choose a place where a missionary is known to be. Communicate with the missionary about the baptisms he has done and then report interesting findings back to your study group.

4. In Acts 18:7–9, the idea of immediacy is not directly stressed. However, what do we know about the time frame from the text?

5. Examine the conversion accounts in the following chapters of the book of Acts: 2, 8, 9, 16, 22. Which ones mention baptism? What other acts of obedience are in these accounts?

6. Mark 16:16 also says, "He who does not believe will be condemned." Does that mean that belief is the only determining factor of salvation? Support your answer.

A Favorite Piece

And speaking of hospitals . . .

was sitting near her bed reading my Bible.

"Read it to me," she requested.

"I sure will, Mom. What part should I read?"

"Just read me whatever it is that you're reading."

So I did:

> The priest shall examine the sore on the skin of the body; and if
> the hair on the sore has turned white, and the sore appears to be
> deeper than the skin of his body, it is a leprous sore.

It was a comforting passage for the bedridden, and this same subject continued for a good five minutes before she decided to go with whatever I was *not* reading at the time.

I was simply trying to read the Bible through, and this happened to be where I was, but as usual, my timing was not good.

Neither was it good during another hospital stay in which my daughter had to mail in a music composition by the national contest deadline. No matter how high you turn the water on in a makeshift studio, namely the bathroom, it's hard to drown out singing in your best projected voice at midnight. Even though the best laid plans were to get it done at home a full day ahead, sometimes hospital emergencies give no warning.

That's the way it was also when my one-year-old downed a full bottle of liquid Tylenol. My husband had questioned if I would be okay with his taking our oldest son along with a missionary to Atlanta to help relocate some printing supplies. It would just be three of our kids, the oldest of whom was five, and me for a few days. What could go wrong?

When you rush out the door to get your kid's stomach pumped, you kind of forget to pack a picnic lunch or supper or breakfast the next day. It was okay for me. A mom can survive anything when her son's liver is on the line, but the other three humans in the room were ready for something a little more sustaining than the popsicles the pink ladies kept bringing. I can't imagine a time in my life when I couldn't call on a hundred or more Christian friends, except for that one day. We had moved to a stateside mission point, and our best friends were with my husband in Atlanta. I could think of other people I had met, but that hospital room had no phone book, even though I requested one often.

You do what you have to do, right? Including freezing during various stays! What floor is this, the test unit for polar bear therapy? The first night, the climate keeps you awake, along with the lights, the announcements, an occasional Brahms Lullaby, and that incessant beeping.

When the nurse's voice comes looming through the wall, you inform her what's going on instead of the other way around by now. "Never mind, I got this," I say, explaining to the wall that it's just occlusion again, and then tell the patient not to move her elbow again.

But by the fifth or sixth night, the recliner that won't recline becomes pretty comfortable after all, and you can sleep through respiratory therapy, housecleaning, vital signs, and minor surgeries. During my sister's turn at caretaking, she was sleeping so good that she jumped up and handed the patient a coffee table when he asked for his walker.

By the seventh night you're completely stir crazy, and the slightest thing can send you into hysterical laughter, such as when you repeatedly call the nurse when you were just trying to change the infomercial.

During my dad's stay last winter, it wasn't enough that our own antics were calling attention to room 823, but as he began to get back to normal—well, his normal is, shall we say, marginal. Nonsense has always been his best friend, so when he would wake in the middle of the night, he would blurt out loudly enough to be heard on the entire wing, some random made-up word. And he also yelled "Warehouse!" every time the phone would ring, or a pager would sound, or there would be a medical alert. The nurses would hover and whisper, but we were ecstatic.

I've learned a lot sitting bedside to one loved one or another through the years. It's overwhelming to think about the medical revolution that has occurred within the walls of those buildings. To think that a kidney could be replaced, digestive systems could be rerouted, and through advanced technology, lungs that have stopped breathing and hearts that have stopped beating could be revived.

Hmmm, with all that ingenuity, you'd think they could do something about the design of that hospital gown.

Whatever Happened to
"Cottage Meetings"
...and That "Joy Bus"?

Bring Back Evangelism

'm not sure who termed these things, but I remember well that bus program of the seventies, and I can think of a whole lot of names for it more suitable than "joy." There was a hole in the floor of our joy bus, and we used to sprawl in our Sunday dresses face-down, and see who could peek through the hole the longest and watch the pavement go by without getting sick. If we were good, we got Chick-O-Sticks candy at the end of the ride. That was the "joy" part.

Then there were the "cottage meetings." This was code for a personal Bible study, but I have never understood the code. I don't think I've ever used the word "cottage" apart from the word "cheese." No one I know lives in a cottage, unless you count the thing Hansel and Gretel found in the woods.

67

To these cottage meetings, I remember my parents taking a big record album, a light projector, and a little plastic cylinder. There was actually a filmstrip inside, but sometimes I wonder if the neighbors thought there was a psychedelic party going on. The filmstrip methodology for evangelism was the best thing since sliced bread, which is especially good with butter, and even though it was modified through the years to VHS and then DVD, it will forever be called the "filmstrips," even to a generation that isn't sure what a filmstrip is.

Of Mice and Women

That brings me to a particularly memorable event. Laura, the silent partner of the evangelism team, sat in a "cottage" watching the "filmstrip" with one eye and a parade of mice with the other. The Pied Piper himself must have stopped overnight at this cottage on his way out of Hamlin and left half his luggage. Praying and remembering her purpose here, Laura was able to make it through the study. Almost. Almost and until one of the mice actually touched her hand on the couch. The silent partner was suddenly silent no more. Laura jumped up and screamed in the middle of the Bible lesson while everyone stared at her. What could she do now? Explain that it was the mice at the risk of embarrassing the homeowners? Make something up at the risk of endangering her own soul? Besides, what could anyone make up that would suffice here? There they were, even the mice's jaws hanging open. Laura did what any of us would do. She straightened her skirt, smiled at the strangers, sat back down, and said, "I'm so sorry. I don't know what came over me."

Um, I think it was a mouse!

Retro-images fill our heads when we think of filmstrips and cottage meetings, but personal evangelism should never slip into

Personal evangelism should never slip into the retro realm.

68

the retro realm. Though the assignment dates back over two thousand years, its renewal is constant.

Final Instructions

Have you ever stood beside the bed of a loved one that you knew you were never going to see on this earth again? Did that person have final words for you—final instructions? Did you flip through channels while he was talking, or did you try to grasp and keep every word? I've got a drawer with a worn piece of paper inside it. At my mother's most lucid hour near the end of her life, she took my hand and gave me some final instructions, and some final blessings. I don't even talk about them much, because they are just my own little treasure. As my mother faded back away into morphine-influenced sub-consciousness, I slipped away, too, to grab a paper and pen before I lost one single word of those instructions. Some were specific, and I keep them to the best of my ability.

In Mark 16 Jesus was going away. He knew that he would never see his disciples in His earthly body again. What were His final instructions? "Go into all the world and preach the gospel to every creature" (v. 15). That was the important message. And Mark, Matthew, and Luke went to get a pen and paper to write it down. The wording varied, but Jesus' final appeal was the same, and we have it on worn pages to remind us.

Daily Practice

From the time the church began in Acts 2, we read in the same chapter that the Lord added to the church daily those who were being saved. Someone was honoring Jesus' final words, and someone was teaching the gospel every single day, and that was to be continued until, according to what Jesus said when He commissioned it, the end of the world (Matthew 28:20 KJV).

I wonder how long it was before man skipped a day in keeping Christ's final instructions. That's the way a permanent deviation usually happens, isn't it? You might skip a day practicing piano, calling a friend, adhering to a diet. Next time you might skip a couple of days. One of those times that you skip multiple days it seems kind of hard to get back to it. Pretty soon you're saying, "I used to play the piano, but I got out of practice," or "I remember her but I haven't thought about her in years," or "Oh yeah, I was on that diet once. I should get back to that."

> And daily in the temple, and in every house, they did not cease teaching and preaching Jesus . . . (Acts 5:42).

Satan's Field Day

I don't really know how long it was before the daily practice in Acts 2 was neglected for a day or two, but I know for many of us it has now become something that we "used to do, "we remember," or "we need to get back to." The thing that was daily, but must have been skipped a day, has now become the thing that is skipped most days, but we're planning to set aside a day for it—soon!

Contrary to popular opinion, because Satan always has a field day with popular opinion, evangelism is not a hard thing to do. Trigonometry is hard; cleaning stables is hard; evangelism is not hard. Peter and John said, "For we cannot but speak the things which we have seen and heard" (Acts 4:20). It came so natural that—I'm going to make English teachers cringe here—they could not *not* do it.

Spiritual Cancer

I can't wait to go to heaven, and for a lot of reasons. Ranking right there at the top, if for no other reason than this one alone: there is no cancer in heaven. I wish we could do something about it on

> Those who are well have no need of a physician, but those who are sick (Luke 5:31).

earth. Imagine that a cure existed for cancer, a real cure that erased it for good. Imagine that I knew what the cure was. Don't you think I'd use every possible channel available to get the message out? It would be all that I could talk about. It would come so natural that I could not *not* do it.

Cancer is a banana split party compared to sin and the eternal hell that awaits the sinner. Sin is a far more widespread disease affecting every single person that has ever lived. We have the cure and it is a simple one! Hallelujah! Why do you think the word *gospel* means "good news"? It's the best news that has ever existed. What keeps us from talking about it, from letting every affected person in on the excitement? It's not so much a question of what, but again, of who. If we don't recognize his efforts, Satan will be successful in quelling our spirit for evangelism, because to him, gospel means bad news.

Satan on the Bus

When we rode that joy bus, we would go out on Saturdays and invite children to be ready for a ride on the bus to church the next day. Some Saturday mornings it was hot, we had gotten up early, and we could already begin to taste the sandwiches that would await our return. Satan had gotten up early, too, and he would ride along convincing us that probably nobody was home, they might still be in bed, there are no vehicles, or they must not have any children. Soon we were just kind of riding around mobile home parks, apartment complexes, and subdivisions rarely doing any kind of evangelism. The joy bus had turned into just a joy ride, until Jamie, nine and fiery, popped up and said, "I'll tell you what's wrong with you people. You don't have no *enthusi-ism*!"

He was right! I'm glad the Samaritan woman didn't behave that way. She had every reason to doubt her success. She was a Samaritan in a culture that degraded Samaritans. She was a woman in a culture that treated women as meager property. And she had an immoral reputation which preceded her.

See for Yourself

I have always been amused at verse 28 of her story in John 4. "She left her waterpot." I didn't know I was a Samaritan, but we must surely have a common gene between us, because she forgot the very

An Extra Helping

Enjoy incredible coffee alongside the milk of the Word. Ask a neighbor to meet with you weekly for coffee. The book of Mark is a fantastic study that will get you through sixteen weeks, and straight to Christ's own words about salvation. Read segments and discuss applications. Never be afraid if you are presented with a difficulty to say, "I don't know the answer, but I know God does. Let's both study that further this week, and come back to it next time."

Here's the incredible coffee part:

Mix 1 quart strong coffee with ⅓ cup sugar. Refrigerate overnight.
Fifteen minutes before the study, add 1 pint chocolate ice cream by the spoonful.
Add ½ cup of your favorite flavored creamer.

Each week try a different flavor of ice cream or creamer. Have cinnamon, cocoa, and nutmeg in shakers for accent.

item that she had come to the well to fill in the first place. And in fact, fully the first half of her conversation with the Lord was solely about that purpose. But something changed near the end of that conversation. She learned some very good news when she realized who the Lord was. Her waterpot was forgotten for a greater purpose. She simply went to the city and, to paraphrase her, she said, "Come and see for yourself." Seeing for yourself is usually the best method. It truly is evangelism when we make the effort to invite someone to simply hear the Word preached so they can see for themselves.

The woman who had very few credentials turned out to be one of the greatest evangelists in scripture. Verse 39 says that many of the Samaritans of that city believed in Jesus simply because of the woman's testimony. Then verse 41 says that more believed after two days of Jesus' own teaching. Success still comes in degrees. Some people are so ready for a Savior in their messed up lives that they are easy to reach with the gospel. Others have been so misguided by men's doctrine that they have to search out the truth for days, and sometimes mull it over for months. They have to literally read and reread Jesus' own directives to see it for themselves. What a blessing when they come to the same ultimate conclusion of the Samaritans in John 4:42,

> Now we believe, not because of what you said, for we ourselves have heard Him and we know that this is indeed the Christ, the Savior of the world.

Three Little Words

The following may seem trite, but simplicity is the beauty of our Christian walk. The enemy is the guy who makes it complicated. Here is a suggestion for a three-phase plan to incorporate evangelism into our lives, and tritely, as promised, the three phases rhyme.

It's the longest poem you'll get from me:

Prayer
Care
Dare

- *Prayer.* From Genesis through Revelation, we are assured time and again that God hears our voice. The God that created everything from sea to sea and the depths within it, who single handedly fed more than a million people in the dessert for forty years, and by the way, is still feeding millions today, is more than capable of answering any genuine petition we have. How is it that we miss praying for specific individuals who need the gospel? It is ultimately their own God-given freewill that determines whether they accept or reject the gospel, but Luke 22:31–32 lets us know that Jesus himself prayed specifically for the individual Simon concerning both his faith and conversion.

  The first step in reaching a friend or acquaintance is bringing that name before God. He is well able to make the arrangements for an open door and open heart.

- *Care.* It often seems that those arrangements involve a situation where we can step in and demonstrate God's care. It may be a joyous occasion, a sad occasion, a complicated one or just a trivial everyday happening. But if you're praying for an open door to share the gospel, God is going to give you one. Walk through it! Call and check in on sick kids, go to extended family members' visitation, bake, drive, contribute, clean, rake, sit—do something! Is there an ulterior motive to the care we exhibit when the need arises? No! And yes. By the command of God, we are to care for all hurting, all hungry, all in crisis (Matthew 25). It is an end within itself. If we never get past the cup of cold water (Matthew 10:42), the coat (Luke 6:29), or the bandaged wounds (Luke 10:34), we have served in Christ's image if we have truly cared for our fellow man. We also need to realize that there is a crisis at hand on a much grander scale than that which even seems devastating. What care have we really shown to those with an earthly finite need, if we ignore their critical, eternal infinite need? If God has opened a door for you to share the gospel, do everything you can in meeting the needs of that person while keeping that door open, and then step up and complete the mission . . .

- *Dare.* Jesus healed, fed, washed feet, cradled children, and soothed tears, but in the end He completed the ultimate mission. It was the most daring thing that has ever been accomplished. It would have been so much easier to live the life of a philanthropist and be remembered as a good friend, but not the unique Savior. But He went through the unthinkable for me. For me!

When we have done all of the good friend part, what is it that keeps us from stepping up and completing the mission? We don't have to be beaten or spit on or crucified. We simply have to share that Someone was and how to get hold of that Good News and wrap our lives around it. What keeps us from doing that?

It's the same guy again.

For God has not given us a spirit of fear, but of power and of love and of a sound mind (2 Timothy 1:7).

If the fear didn't come from God, guess who it came from. Satan is perfectly happy for us to help homeless shelters and children's hospitals and give away as many cars as Oprah has as long as we don't mention how to escape hell while doing it.

- It is Satan who is telling you that you don't know enough. But you knew enough to obey the gospel.

Evangelism:

Prayer

Care

Dare

- It is Satan who is telling you they will think you're a fanatic.
- It is Satan who is telling you they will not be interested.

Back to 2 Timothy 1:7:

- It is God who is giving you a spirit of power—you can do this! It is God who is giving you a spirit of love—how can you not do this?
- It is God who is giving you a sound mind—you are capable of imparting the truth in scriptures!

Swallow hard, look your friend in the eye, and say, "I was wondering if you might like to study the Bible together." Dare.

It's the best way to get "enthusi-ism."

> *How then shall they call on Him in whom they have not*
> *believed? And how shall they believe in Him of whom they have*
> *not heard? And how shall they hear without a preacher?*
> —Romans 10:14

Soul Food

1. Think of a time when you were afraid to ask someone to study the Bible, but you did anyway. How did that turn out? If you have never asked someone to study the Bible, think of another of God's commands that you were afraid to do but went through with. How did that one turn out? How can that give you confidence to be involved in personal evangelism on a regular basis?

2. Have you experienced the death of a person particularly close to you? Do you remember the last words that person said to you? How have they impacted you? Do you think the fact that Jesus'

command to evangelize was His last command on earth makes it any more significant?

3. What do you see as the greatest hindrance to us in evangelizing to the degree we should?

4. If you never worked on the bus program, find someone who has. Find out what they think were the greatest strengths and weaknesses of this program. Why have most churches stopped engaging in bus ministry? What is keeping you from initiating a similar program?

5. If we had a cure for cancer, we would use every means possible to communicate it to the world. Now list five of your most successful suggestions for getting the word out. Then consider each and determine which are already being used for evangelism and which could be used. How can you be personally involved in using one of those five most promising channels?

A Favorite Piece

And speaking of homeowners . . .

"A soft answer turns away wrath" (Proverbs 15:1). That much we know. But tell me, what kind of answer turns away a sales call? I've tried pretty much everything imaginable, including "I have a communicable disease that travels through the cell phone," only to be asked if I'd like to buy an extended warranty for the disease in six easy payments.

My daughter's answer was my favorite. When asked if the homeowner was available, she looked over at me while

I was peeling an orange and decided to say that I was a little busy right now. However, she got her tongue tied and said, "She's little bitty right now; could you call back later?" Now that was a blatant lie. "A little busy" would have been somewhat honest, being that orange peels are demanding. But nothing could have been further from the truth nor provoked more laughter in the kitchen than that I was little bitty, particularly considering that I was about to grow even further by the size of one navel orange.

Because we are not so good at thinking of honest reasons not to talk—"talk" meaning try to squeeze half-syllables in like yo-, we-, hu- —and we certainly can't in good conscience give dishonest ones, our only strategy is, "Don't answer that!" And it somehow seems unfair that we are paying forty-nine dollars a month to have something we are afraid to use.

On certain days when I feel it especially necessary to answer the phone—such as when I am expecting the dog groomer to call and say Buladean is misbehaving and must be picked up, which is likely—we have a policy to hang up if after saying hello, we count to two fast and no one has said anything. This is because we know that at "People-Who-Call-to-Sell-Stuff-You-Can't-Afford International Inc.," no one is expecting anyone to actually say hello because everyone in the entire solar system has Caller ID, which is another word for a little box that alerts you that "People-Who-Call-to-Sell-Stuff-You-Can't-Afford International Inc." is calling you, except for us, and so when someone actually does say hello, the sales staff is caught off guard and there is complete hysteria until someone at PWCTSSYCA International Inc. finally grabs the receiver and nervously mispronounces your name.

My mom got one once who said, "Good evening, may I please speak to 941 Lynn Dale Lane?" to which my mom said, "Excuse me?" to which the sales caller said, "Oh, I'm sorry, I mean can I please speak to Lee Holder?"

"She's a little bitty right now . . ."

78

The "count to two fast" policy would work pretty well were it not for the fact that my own father, for as long as I can remember, has failed to respond, when someone answers the phone, for at least two seconds. So after I hang up on what I think to be three consecutive telemarketers before they can say anything, it is inevitably my father the fourth time, who says, "We got disconnected three times."

As Christians we sometimes discuss how we can avoid being kidnapped on the phone while still being kind and patient with the callers. It's a dilemma, but I like Pearl's approach. Pearl takes out her hearing aid when the phone rings, so she literally cannot hear anything. Pearl's end of the conversation goes like this, "Hello? Hello? What? What? I can't hear you. I can't understand a thing you're saying. What?" This successfully ends the sales call but proved to be quite frustrating when I called Pearl to see if she could help provide food after a funeral.

"Hello, Pearl, wondering if you could help us out."

"What? What? I can't hear you."

"This is Celine."

"Not being mean, hon, just can't hear you."

"Can you make a casserole for Thursday?"

"Castrol? No, my son handles all that. If you're selling oil, he won't be back until Friday. Goodbye—"

"Pearl, wait, I'm talking about for the funeral."

"I've already done preplanning."

"Let's see then. Can you just make rolls?"

"What? Mae Croyle? I have her number, but she goes to the beauty shop on Tuesdays."

"Okay, Pearl. Bye, Pearl. Have a good day, Pearl."

"Who?"

Now the telemarketer I mentioned before who accidentally asked to speak to our address instead of a person had obviously not graduated from Inconvenient Callers University (ICU) where you cannot receive a diploma until you have mastered the following:

1. Be able to speak a minimum of 1500 words without taking a breath.

2. Be able to convince someone that what he is now paying for anything is way more than he can currently afford, and so what he should do to save money is *buy something else!*

3. Ask someone to take a survey, and then give her a multiple choice question to which there is no correct answer.

4. Call someone thousands of times every week, each time telling her that this is her last chance to renew something she doesn't have.

5. Assume everyone has credit card debt.

6. Be able to calculate the exact moment every homeowner is about to put the first bite of supper in her mouth.

7. Be able to divide any price by a number whose quotient will exactly equal the price of a cup of coffee.

And I don't know about you, but I'm the luckiest person on the planet. Last week, I received a call that I had won something. Wouldn't you know? After all the Super Bowl tickets I've registered for and all the drawings for the giant stockings and Easter baskets at the supermarket, I finally won something!

And it was a cemetery plot.

Whatever Happened to
Being Taken Out
for a Whippin'?

Bring Back Mama

Well, that's one I don't miss, at least on the receiving "end." When we got thrown over the shoulder and hustled out the back via the center aisle, we knew when we got to the nursery it wouldn't be to get in the floor and play with Lincoln Logs. Often cries of "no, no, no" accompanied the escort out which could be particularly embarrassing if the congregation was singing, "Would You Live for Jesus?"

Once an elder by the name of George Hibbett was standing in the back of an auditorium in Florence, Alabama, when a young boy was taken out for the correction process. As one last appeal for mercy, the toddler yelled, "Help me, George!"

I think everyone heard it, and I also think it was the last thing they heard that morning.

That Shoe Doesn't Fit

What we in the South have referred to as the "whippin'" has all but disappeared, not only from the church assembly but also from the school and, most regrettably, from the home. I looked up the nursery rhyme I could most relate to, *The Old Woman in the Shoe*, a few years ago—you know, the one who had so many children she didn't know what to do. It's not that I'm not incredibly grateful for every little soul; it's just where I would find myself some days, not knowing what to do. I do know what the old woman did. She

An Extra Helping

Experience the following after-school snack and conversation:

Honey Balls

(A friend's mother served these up to children in an old wooden schoolhouse.)

1 cup honey
1 cup peanut butter
2 cups powdered milk
Corn flakes

Mix the first three ingredients together, make into small balls, and roll them in crushed corn flakes.

These go well with milk, two questions, and a round of a favorite card game.

The questions: What was the highlight of your day? What was the low point of your day?

spanked them all soundly and sent them to bed. But when I looked up the nursery rhyme, the words had been changed. She no longer spanked them soundly, but instead, kissed them soundly ("Old Woman Who Lived in a Shoe"). I don't even know what that means. I have been kissed by my husband, my children, grandparents, countless aunts and uncles, and puppies. I can think of a lot of different adjectives to describe those different kisses, but I have never once had a kiss and thought, *Wow, that was sound!*

But I guess those who wished to be politically correct—another phrase that I don't get—removed any hint of corporal punishment, which left the old woman in the shoe in the same state that most teachers and parents, with little recourse, find themselves, again not knowing what to do.

I recently heard a church deacon speaking before the Lord's supper, of all things, about this topic. He publicly recognized that the Proverbs advise parents to physically administer punishment, but he struggled with it (out loud to an assembly) because he kept thinking, *What would Jesus do?*

For whom the Lord loves He chastens, and scourges every son whom He receives (Hebrews 12:6).

God's Love Disciplines Me

Jesus would do the right thing; Jesus would do the loving thing. And Proverbs 13:24 says that is prompt discipline with a rod. Jesus was God in the flesh, and scriptures assure us that God loves us enough to correct us as a loving father does (Proverbs 3:12, Hebrews 12:6–7, Revelation 3:19), and Hebrews 12:6 specifically says a scourging. Why would God the Son be any less loving than God the Father?

A couple of years ago, an archbishop in Louisiana banned Catholic schools from administering paddlings. And you will never guess who protested the ruling: the students! Yes, the student body turned out in huge numbers with the message, "Leave St. Aug alone" (Carr). They recognized that the reason their education was superior to that in other schools was that student behavior was manageable. They felt safe where there were enforced boundaries.

Gary Smalley recounts the following in his and Ted Cunningham's book, *As Long as We Both Shall Live: Experiencing the Marriage You've Always Wanted*:

> My mother said she never spanked because her first child died of blood poisoning and she had spanked her two weeks before she died. She made my father promise to never spank any one of their five remaining children . . .
>
> Once my father caught me in a serious infraction as a young boy. From his firm voice I knew that I was in trouble. Later he said he would let me off without punishing me if I promised not to do it again. I actually told him that I needed a spanking, but he wouldn't do it. There was something in me that wanted to be corrected.
>
> I found the same permissiveness in school. Once a teacher caught me passing notes in the third grade after warning me of the consequences if I didn't stop. She sent me to the principal. He talked to me for a while, told me I needed to shape up, than said that he was going to spank me. I thought he really meant business, but about fifteen minutes later, he said he was going to give me another chance if I promised not to pass notes again. Of course, I promised the world, but inwardly I can remember being disappointed that he didn't follow through (Cunningham and Smalley 52–53).

The swatted child spread his arms wide open, and wrapped them around the dress of that teacher, and said, "I love you!"

A Hankering for a Spanking

I was in a Bible class with a little boy named Michael who came to church with his grandmother. His home was a mess, and he had never really been disciplined. When it came to his behavior, he held the reins. Looking back as adults, we all have hilarious memories of the things Michael did in Bible class from climbing out the window, to throwing crayons across the room, to standing up and telling the teacher what he would and wouldn't do. One day the teacher snatched him up by the arm and swatted his bottom before she had time to talk herself out of it. There was silence, and most of us were trying to decide whether to hide or run. And then the child spread his arms wide open, and wrapped them around the dress of that teacher, and said, "I love you!"

I wish every parent could understand the longing that a child has to be disciplined in a healthy way. My heart hurts for any child who is beaten or abused, and I will do everything in my power to prevent that from happening or to rescue any child from the situation. But a firm spanking, when needed and administered in a loving and consistent way, becomes a blessing to the child in developing lifelong character and understanding the consequences of choices and behavior.

> As is the Mother, so is her daughter
> (Ezekiel 16:44 KJV).

Where's Mama?

But it's not just the corporal punishment debate that I'm concerned about in this chapter. When I wonder whatever happened to being taken out for a whippin', I glance around and wonder, "Where is the person who is responsible for those trips out back to the nursery? Paul Faulkner and Carl Brecheen titled their 1979 book, *Whatever*

Happened to Mom, Dad, and the Kids? (Brecheen, Carl and Paul Faulkner). And since I'm primarily writing to ladies, I narrow the question: Whatever happened to Mom?

The position of Mama may just be the most powerful position in the world. Generations are steered toward emotional, physical, and spiritual prosperity by the influence of one good mother, and generations are drowning in tumultuous depravity because of the influence of one bad one. Yet popular media shows those dedicated to motherhood as the weakest of all living.

A television show which recently had a long, successful run was titled *Desperate Housewives.* The famous opening sequence, which displays male-female roles depicted in art through the centuries, was designed to "evoke the show's quirky spirit and playful flouting of women's traditional role in society" (Desperate Housewives). It's no accident that those in the series most dedicated to perfecting motherhood yield the most diabolical urchins. What's the conclusion here? Perhaps the writers have some appeal as humorists, but I'm certainly not endorsing it! Make no mistake, though. There is a statement, and it's not in favor of godly mothers investing their lives in their children.

Conversely, several years ago *Christian Woman* magazine asked readers to share their favorite memory of coming home from school as they were growing up. I was surprised at the number of answers that revolved around not what was there, but who was there. Memories of homemade snacks and listening ears. I remember seeing my own mother appear as I topped a hill on my way home from the bus stop. She had a glass of tea in one hand and a glass of lemonade in the other. She met me halfway, and then turned and accompanied me the rest

> Popular media depicts those dedicated to motherhood as the weakest of all living.

> . . . I call to remembrance the genuine faith that is in you, which dwelt first in your grandmother Lois and your mother Eunice . . . (2 Timothy 1:5).

of the way as we soaked up the ice-cold drinks in the hot afternoon sun. Whatever happened to that?

Bring Back Mama!

Isn't it the most awesome God-granted responsibility we could attain? To know that God has placed a valuable soul in your womb and then laid him at your nursing breast and given you eighteen years to cradle, to heal, to guide, to instruct, and to marvel. God elevated you to that position, and the world is chanting to get off the pedestal for no other reason than the world wants your son or daughter.

Who was it that God entrusted with His own Son? Who was it that He carefully handpicked to nurture Him all through His earthly struggles? Mother. She was the only human being who was there at both His humble birth and His cruel death. She was Mother.

My favorite author apart from the Holy Spirit is Dr. Seuss. He had a way of driving home points that were deeper than just green eggs and hat-wearing cats. One of his characters, a bird named Mayzie, neglected to sit on her egg because she was too busy flitting around Palm Springs and everywhere else, so Horton the elephant took over for her. When the bird hatched weeks later, she not only had wings, but a little trunk and huge ears. He had cared for the little egg, and the hatchling had become like him (Seuss).

Elephants and Lost Boys

It's no wonder that generations are forsaking the morality of their parents. No wonder they look more like the elephant than the bird. Children will take on the characteristics of those who wielded the greatest influence over them, and with children—with all of us— that is spelled t-i-m-e. Don't let the elephant sit on your egg.

Disney's version of *Peter Pan* includes a song called *Your Mother and Mine* (Beaumont). It talks about the angel voice and the helping hand and the gentle whispers, all sung to a group of little boys who had never known a mother. That's why they are "lost boys."

Any child who doesn't experience a mother in all of these ways truly is a lost boy or a lost girl. Peter Pan could manage by hearing about mothers without really having one, only because Peter Pan would never grow up. Those who do grow up need a mother to get them there in one piece.

Before I get away from elephants and Disney movies, I have to mention *Dumbo*. It was my firstborn son's first favorite video. While he probably liked the clowns jumping out of the blazing high-rise buildings best, I was particularly partial to the mother elephant scooping up her baby and rocking him as she sang:

> If they knew sweet little you,
> They'd end up loving you, too.
> All those same people who scold you,
> What they'd give just for
> The right to hold you.
> From your head to your toes
> You're not much, goodness knows.
> But you're so precious to me
> Cute as can be, baby of mine (Noyes).

Whose baby will not face the bitter reality one day of a world that measures worth in the shape of his ears, the size of her nose, the measure of his height, the brand of her clothes, or most prominently, the thickness of his wallet? The survivors will be the ones who have been scooped up and held tight, valued as a gift from God, mothered.

Are You Mother?

A woman lay in the bed of a small room down the hall of a nursing home in Anniston, Alabama. She was not aged or wrinkled like the other residents. She was a young lady trapped in her own body, mangled in a car crash when she was seventeen. She had suffered severe brain damage, and no one knew if she really knew who she was. But she had a strong voice and a tireless persistence. It was as if she had only one thought; she could say three words: "Are you Mother?" Sometimes softly, sometimes elongated, often deafeningly loud and desperate, "Are you Mother?" When she was robbed of everything else including her dignity, she wanted only one thing . . . Mother.

Do you have a unique opportunity to be someone to a child that no one else on the face of this earth can be? Do you have a short time to shape a life destined for greatness in God's kingdom? Are you Mother?

Lose Big

I once watched a morning show in which a motivational author chided those who forfeited their own pursuits because, at that time, they were focused on others. She specifically said she was tired of hearing things like, "I'm focused on my kids right now," that this was an excuse, and that people who say such things are losers. With this kind of rhetoric, no wonder the housewives are desperate! She pled with us to, instead, follow the dream.

What she didn't understand was, *this is the dream.* Giving one hundred percent attention to our children's spiritual growth and well-being this side of the Jordan is causing the real estate value on the other side to skyrocket. We have a solid grasp on the ultimate dream. But she got one thing right. We—the mothers, the child investors—are losers.

> *Whoever loses his life for My sake will find it.*
> —Matthew 16:25

Soul Food

1. How have you seen attitudes toward spanking a child change through the years? Watch an old black-and-white sitcom with children on it. Is there discipline in the show? Watch a current sitcom with children on it. How do these shows differ? Do you think these shows impact parenting practices or do you think parenting practices influence the shows?

2. This chapter cites two proverbs that deal with disciplining children. List other proverbs dealing with that subject.

3. Do you agree that there are times when children really long for a spanking? When they do not get it, how do you think this plays out?

4. Have you ever seen a child seem particularly grateful for a spanking? If so, recall that memory and share it if you are in a group study.

5. Read Dr. Seuss' *Horton Hatches the Egg*. Make a list of the parallels you find to human parenting and how Christian parents can benefit from the analogy.

6. Sometimes it is difficult for parents with young children to manage during worship assembly. Being "taken out for a whippin'," while sometimes necessary, is not suggested as the first recourse. If you are not focused on very young children of your own, pick

someone out in your congregation who has young children, and share a pew this Sunday. Make it your goal to engage the little ones so Mom can be blessed by the sermon. Plan ahead how you can best accomplish this, and be patient if they derail your plans.

7. In scripture, how were generations affected specifically by one good mother? Also, what bad mother affected generations to come, and how?

A Favorite Piece

And speaking of mothers ... and fathers ...

Mother's Day is fun. You get to eat out at your kids' favorite restaurant which automatically means a prize in your meal. But it would be much better if it weren't on Sunday, or if church could start, say, at 12:30. Your kids bring you breakfast in bed, meaning sixty percent of a Pop-Tart, and your first thought is, "How much would it be to just get a new toaster instead of trying to dig down there with the ice pick to retrieve the other forty percent—again?" But that is quickly interrupted by your second thought, "Whoa! 8:12!"

"This Pop-Tart is wonderful. Indiana Jones flavor has always been my favorite. Now get in the shower!" And then it starts.

"I don't have any clean underwear."

"Where's my other sock?"

"Can I wear flip-flops?"

"Do these match if I fold this part under?"

"Do I have to wear a belt again?"

"Where's the lint brush? Never mind, I'll vacuum it."

Then somehow you find that you have actually made it to and through Bible study and worship with the worst thing being that you put the fingernail polish on the run in your hose at the precise moment your husband cleared the railroad tracks, so that ninety percent of the congregation has now asked if you had another wobbly ladder incident at your house. And there is that shirt you're going to have to retrieve from the vacuum cleaner later.

Then comes the good part. Your husband is prepared for the event and has applied Luke 6:31 to its fullest: "Whatsoever I would want my wife to give unto me, that will I give to her also." Men, for all their magical worth, have tunnel vision when it comes to what a person would like for a gift. I should say aisle vision, consisting of everything on Aisle 15 of the home improvement store. Their criteria are sweet, consisting of: a) Will she like it? b) Does anyone know if she already has one of these? and c) How much horsepower?

The problem with Mother's Day and Father's Day is that we have them mixed up. Fathers are getting things in frilly bags with tissue paper and Mother's are getting things wrapped in—I promise—a fitted sheet and duct tape. Wouldn't it be better if the women planned the thing for the women and the men planned the thing for the men? That is what makes the ladies' days and men's breakfasts work. We plan them for ourselves. Can you imagine otherwise? The marquee would read: *Bloom Where You Are Fertilized, Let the Beauty of Scrap Iron Be Seen in Me,* or *I Can Do All Things If You Give Me Enough Drill Bits.*

For all the hoopla of Mother's Day, Father's Day is probably more fun. Dad doesn't care what we wear. He will go if you pin a boutonnière to a sweat suit, as long as the flower's not pink. He doesn't care where we eat as long as they super-size and give free refills. He doesn't care what you give him, as long as you don't tie those gift bag handles with curly ribbon that won't

> *I come home to find clean-up has consisted of a round with the leaf blower.*

come off with his pocket knife. His only comment is "Thank you" and "How much did this cost?" Dads put us to shame in the area of contentment.

If it weren't for dads, would we really ever have any fun? Would any of us have ever enjoyed the occasional thrill of a good head-whacking by the ceiling fan blade during an old-fashioned round of toss-the-kid with no regard to the marble floor below?

I looked out my window a few years back as I was washing dishes, and there was a mom circling the block with her five-year-old on a tricycle. He was bundled up for those occasional early April winds, and geared a helmet, kneepads, and elbow pads. What fun as his mom kept one hand on his shoulder and the other on the adjacent stroller!

I put the dishes aside and went to peer out the garage window at our own family fun. There they were: my two-year-old coasting down the driveway on a bike with training wheels in nothing but a diaper while Dad occasionally turned from washing the car to spray him with the water hose. They were both delighted.

Yeah, dads are more fun. The kids jump up and down with joy if I have a board meeting or ladies' night out, and leave the supper duties to dad. They start scrounging the drawer for the pizza coupon before I can get out the door. They eat off the cardstock because they can't find the paper plates, and I come home to find clean-up has consisted of a round with the leaf blower.

When writing columns, I always struggle with Father's Day. My dad was so extremely that—a dad, with such pronounced right-brain dominance that no sensible editor can believe my tribute to him. It sounds like I'm making it up. It really is true that he came home from work every day, hung his suit coat on a tree branch, and without a word, pitched a hundred horse shoes, no more or no less, before coming in the house. It's true that our barbecue grill was an adjustable, rotating model made of a garbage can and three chains hanging from a pine tree. It's true that we had a swing with a thirty-foot chain attached to two trees at the edge of the woods.

My dad made everything including soap—which my friends were afraid to use because it looked like botulism that had already happened—and a Ferris wheel for the school carnival.

He always had—and still has—a sing-while-you-work attitude, but his substituted lyrics consist mainly of "goo-shot, goo-shot" and "round and round." He will be eighty-seven this year—quit doing the math. He had me extremely late in life!—and I worry that at his age, someone will mistake his off-the-wall eccentrics for some age-related onset of a mental condition. But I shake my head. Not yet. Not yet. He's always been that way.

He has always set items on the top of the car and made mental notes of how long they would ride. He has always done short versions of Easter egg hunts year round with the dog, only hiding pieces of hot dog wieners instead of eggs. But his protective, nourishing, tender-hearted fatherhood qualities have always prevailed over his would-be complete insanity.

Recently, he had signs of a squirrel breaking and entering his garage. He decided to plaster the hole, but the moment he started to do so, his villain peered around the corner from inside the hole with sad eyes. My dad, as we knew he would be, was taken in. He put off the patching job until he knew the squirrel was safe outside the walls. The next morning, the squirrel came to his glass sliding door to ask for a second chance. They are now friends, as with the orphaned birds, the pregnant alley cat, and the abandoned peacock who forever has a homemade plaque on Dad's wall as a tribute to their friendship.

There are few words on Father's Day to summarize the impact of a dad so left of center, yet so right on target, but I will try these:

"Goo-shot, goo-shot. Round and round."

Whatever Happened to Sunday-Go-to-Meetin' Clothes

Bring Back the Spiritual Change of Clothes

We're now defining dress clothes as the jeans without holes in them. I'm certainly not devoting a chapter to dress code since 1 Samuel 16:7 tells us that "man looks at the outward appearance, but the Lord looks at the heart." And if we get anything out of the first four verses of James 2, we're not going to worry about who makes the best-dressed list. It's an aisle, not a runway.

I do believe with all my heart that we should dress modestly in the worship assembly, but not just because it's the worship assembly. I think we ought to dress modestly at the ball field, the grocery store, washing the car in the driveway, and mowing the front lawn. We should be just as much about dressing appropriately for God the other 164 hours we spend with Him each week as we are about the four inside the church walls.

I also believe that whoever invented pantyhose should be forced to sit through eighteen hours of an off-key opera solo in an un-air-conditioned building sitting on a broken bicycle seat next to an experienced telemarketer, so that he or she could more deeply appreciate the comfort we have all been blessed with due to his or her creative efforts.

> Put on the new man which was created according to God, in true righteousness and holiness (Ephesians 4:24).

Get Your Clothes On!

But back in my parents' dating era, church clothes were on a different level than all other clothing. They were Sunday-go-to-meeting clothes, and it was a shame if you got a spot of dirt or grease on them or, even worse, a tear in the fabric. The pews were slats with cracks of varying widths. If you got your dress caught in a narrow slat, you might tear it if you weren't careful. One morning the lady in front of my daddy wasn't careful. As the congregation stood for the invitation song, she stood but her dress didn't.

Unfortunately, Daddy is a very helpful person. He found himself picking up pieces of the seat of her dress, and trying to put them back in place. He also found himself realizing what he was doing and at once, throwing all the pieces down on the pew. I heard he was the color of a cherry popsicle that day, and he still doesn't like to talk about it, even though the pews have long been replaced and no one can even remember the lady's name.

In the New Testament, there seems to be no given dress code for Sunday that wouldn't apply to every day of the week. However, there is a mandatory outfit that we read about in Galatians 3:27: "For as many of you as were baptized into Christ have put on Christ." We have had a spiritual change of clothes. We have put Him on, never to take Him off again. What a remarkable difference that one change has made. The old outfit:

> For we ourselves were also once foolish, disobedient, deceived, serving various lusts and pleasures, living in malice and envy, hateful and hating one another (Titus 3:3).

> Sounds like every Dr. Phil episode I've ever seen.

> But when the kindness and the love of God our Savior toward man appeared—[Here comes the new outfit]—according to His mercy He saved us (Titus 3:3–5).

> Bring back the change of clothes.

Ever Going to Change That Shirt?

If you've ever been to Bible camp, you know that the youngest campers, free from the reminders of their parents for a week, never open their suitcase unless it's to put a souvenir bug in it. It never occurs to them to change clothes. They get up Tuesday with the same shirt they had on Monday, and then Wednesday . . . and Thursday. Pretty soon they smell pretty much like the dead fish in the lake, and look like Pig Pen, the *Peanuts* character. A cloud of dry dirt is stirred up every time you brush against them in the lunch line. Sometimes a counselor will tactfully make a suggestion, "When are you going to change that shirt? You've had it on since Watergate!" The really conscientious, compliant camper will obey the counselor . . . by turning it inside out.

We are perplexed by the behavior, being that the child has an entire suitcase of clean clothes. Hasn't he spent enough of his life in that same shirt? Haven't we?

For we have spent enough of our past lifetime in doing the will
of the Gentiles—when we walked in lewdness, lusts, drunken-
ness, revelries, drinking parties, and abominable idolatries
(1 Peter 4:3).

Lewdness? Drinking parties? I think some of us have forgotten
to change our shirts when we became Christians. And some of
us, at best, have just tried to disguise it by turning it inside out. It
may be an attempt to look different from the outside, but we're still
wrapped up in the same old thing from the inside.

An Extra Helping

Make a birthday dress for a little girl in your realm of influence,
with a keepsake card that reads, "A new dress is fun to put on. One
day, you will put on Christ, and that will be the best dress of all!"
Pretty pillowcase dress instructions:

1. Hold a pillowcase up to a child approximately the same size as
   the recipient to get the length you want. (When you add the
   band at the end, the dress will become longer, so take that into
   consideration.) Cut the amount you need to take off from the
   closed end of the pillowcase. This is the part you don't need.

2. Fold the pillowcase so that the two seams are together, and there
   is a crease down the length of it. Cut a small U-shape at the
   seams-edge on the end you just cut open to create two armholes
   when unfolded. Finish the armholes by serging or hemming.

3. Fold the unfinished top down to the inside a fraction of an inch
   and press; fold down again 1 inch; press and sew to make casing. Run colorful ribbon through the casing to tie at shoulders.
   Cut a strip of a coordinating fabric measured to go all the way
   around the bottom of the dress, plus enough to make a seam on
   one side. Hem the strip, sew a seam in the strip with right sides
   together; attach to the bottom of the dress by sewing one edge of
   it (right sides together) to the edge of dress; turn and press.

It May Look Weird to You, But . . .

As forgiven Christians, we've spent enough of our lives doing the Gentile thing. We've got a new outfit now, and it should be obvious to everyone. Keep reading: "Wherein they think it strange that ye run not with them to the same excess of riot" (1 Peter 4:4 KJV). When we put on Christ, we suddenly looked different from the rest of the world. Our Sunday-go-to-meetin' clothes have become our Monday-go-to-work and Tuesday-go-to-school and Thursday-go-to-tennis and—you get the idea! We wear Christ at all times and in all places.

> What shall we say then? Shall we continue in sin that grace may abound? Certainly not! How shall we who died to sin live any longer in it? (Romans 6:1–2).

Don't stop reading there because the next verse is one so parallel to the one about putting on Christ.

> Or do you not know [Don't you get it?] that as many of us as were baptized into Christ Jesus were baptized into His death? (Romans 6:3).

Time for Change

As the *Alcoholics Anonymous* adage goes, "Change playgrounds and change playmates." Change your shirt! When we continue to walk like the world, talk like the world, and rub shoulders with the world, what are we thinking? We have a suitcase full of new clothes, and we'd rather smell like dead fish.

Paul gives us another don't-you-get-it warning in 1 Corinthians 6: 9–11,

> We have a suitcase full of new clothes, and we'd rather smell like dead fish.

> Do you not know that the unrighteous will not inherit the king-
> dom of God? Do not be deceived. Neither fornicators, nor idolaters,
> nor adulterers, nor homosexuals, nor sodomites, nor thieves,
> nor covetous, nor drunkards, nor revilers, nor extortioners will
> inherit the kingdom of God. And such were some of you.

There we were in that stinking shirt. And the next word is my
favorite conjunction of all: *but.*

> But you were washed, but you were sanctified, but you were justi-
> fied in the name of the Lord Jesus and by the Spirit of our God.

We had a change of clothes when we put on Christ in baptism.
And that change has allowed us access to an amazing inheritance,
the kingdom of God. Don't give it up. Notice his caution light in the
middle of the verse: "Do not be deceived."

Don't Take It Off!

The new outfit is conspicuous. Hello, we knew that when we put it
on. First Peter 4:4 has established that. But don't go back to the old
one. If it weren't so easy to slip back into the familiar world of sin,
the Holy Spirit wouldn't give us so many caution flags about it.

Satan works extra hours to win back those he has lost to Christ.
He can dress up sin as compromise, tolerance, or a weekend of fun.
But he delivers traps, addictions, tangled webs and regret.

In the analogy of the outfit, Satan makes it seem that the world
is walking around in soft blue jeans and furry slippers, but the truth
is . . .

What they really have on is tight pantyhose.

And do not present your members as instruments of unrighteousness
to sin, but present yourselves to God as being alive from the dead,
and your members as instruments of righteousness to God.
—Romans 6:13

Soul Food

1. Titus 3:3 lists characteristics that once described us. Which of these in the list is it easiest for us to fall back into? What about for you personally?

2. What do you like best about getting a new outfit? What parallels can you draw between the benefits of a new outfit and the benefits of a new life in Christ?

3. Read James 2:1–4. Do you think this passage is relevant to our dress in assemblies in our culture today? Do you think it has a broader application than just dress in worship? Disregard the chapter division, a man-made expedient, and consider whether this is a continued discussion of James 1:27.

A Favorite Piece

And speaking of dressy clothes . . .

Here comes Peter Cottontail; there goes the bank account. I have always really looked forward to all the holidays, especially the ones where we got out of school. I thought, for instance, that Columbus was a TV detective in a trench coat, but I always celebrated his birthday in grand style. The best holidays, though, involve chocolate, which is why Easter is a biggie. The joy of Easter truly extends beyond the day and into many nights when I raid the baskets after bedtime.

The chocolate is fabulous; the fashion demands? Not so much. Easter, also known as New Expensive Dress Sunday, can be exciting when you have a six-month-old first daughter that you've been smocking for since you were eleven. It's an altogether different thing when there are six of you to clothe, one of whom is a sixteen-year-old male who discriminates between dress clothes and casual clothes by how many holes are in the jeans.

Maybe he's extreme, but it's just that way with the boys from the beginning. It's kind of difficult when Easter rolls around if all your girl friends have baby girls except for you. Their little ones totter into the church building looking somewhat ethereal, complete with a halo of baby's breath entwined with grapevine. Fairy glitter literally falls from their hems in the shapes of hearts and stars. I wonder for a moment if I had a wreck on the way to church and am being met with cherubs to escort me Home.

Then there's my kid. It's kind of unfair that the closest thing they make for boys to the ethereal department is a brown and navy argyle sweater vest, which he loudly protested in favor of the batman cape. Still he looks kind of cute, even with the fresh Count Chocula stain on the front, as he plows his way through the angelic host like a John Deere backhoe rooting its way through the Rose Garden.

I guess we should be thankful for boys' wear—no fancy handwork, no French seams, no going cross-eyed at 1:00 A.M. on Easter Eve trying to smock a pony hoof. Just a 28.95 sweater and nine dollars in Wet One wipes. My friend Sarah just couldn't succumb to the Y chromosome thing. She wanted to hand-embroider just one more frilly outfit, so that Easter she compromised by making a true big boy's dress shirt, but adding a pastel embroidered choo-choo to the back. I didn't think he'd wear it.

He plows his way through the angelic host like a John Deere backhoe rooting its way through the Rose Garden.

He did. Under a jacket for the entirety of Sunday school and "big church." Sarah pled with him until practically no one was left in the building but the janitorial staff. He finally bargained to take off the jacket if he could swing from the sound booth to the pulpit on a drop cord. Deal! He actually survived, but no such luck for the shirt.

It's just an unwritten law. The more assets you sink into imperial batiste cotton and chiffon, the more quickly those assets liquidate in the form of recycled baby formula and mashed peas. Also, the more expensive the designer purse of the elder's wife admiring the smocking, the nearer in proximity it is to the liquidation.

I'm glad Easter's about a lot more than the clothing catastrophes, and that at least part of the holiday revolves around something sensible, like hard-boiling eight dozen eggs for a family of six, and then putting five coffee mugs full of permanent dye on a mahogany-finish table with the four people who are solely responsible for the total collapse of the pantry shelving system.

"You mean we're going to do this *inside?*" my husband asked.

The next year we thought we might substitute with the candy eggs which come already colored and individually wrapped. That was before we tasted them. "What's in this?" my husband asked, "Organic linoleum?"

As the hour for Peter Cottontail's arrival nears, we prepare by leaving empty, plastic ice cream buckets out, containers that would hold large amounts of milk chocolate. My children were surprised to learn that other children have brightly colored baskets woven in Taiwan with disproportionately long handles which serve no other purpose than to strew candy and eggs all across a lawn so that a more fortunate child can find them. They didn't know other kids have shreds of pink plastic grass lining their baskets which serve a better, more decorative purpose of wrapping around the vacuum cleaner belt until the thing won't turn.

"How come we don't have baskets like that, and pretty grass?" they ask us.

"We're going green," we explain, "It's why we save ice cream buckets all year."

There are many more memories that go along with the holiday: memories that involve licking the fluorescent icing and coconut grass off the cupcakes before throwing the jelly beans away, or at your sister; memories of 3:00 A.M. panic at who might be in the middle of the dog fight in the front yard in which pink fur is reported to be flying. And countless memories of near straightjacket encounters with plastic eggs that are designed to be snapped apart, but not back together.

We love Easter. There are families at church that we see only once a year. We watch *It's the Easter Beagle, Charlie Brown* and read the complete works of Beatrix Potter. We eat potato salad heavy on blue-tinted hardboiled eggs until we're pretty much shaped like one. And when all is said and done, we have spent another Sunday reflecting on the sacrifice of an amazing Savior on our behalf, and His miraculous resurrection—something we reflect on, by the way, fifty-two Sundays a year.

And that's really the best part. All the rest is just chocolate.

Whatever Happened to Singing Twelve Verses of "Just as I Am"?

Bring Back the Tears of Joy

Remember when an invitation song was about inviting people to respond to the gospel? When people filed past you to get to the aisle, you didn't assume it was because they really couldn't wait to get to the bathroom. You knew it was because they really couldn't wait to get to Jesus. Then the preacher would signal to the song leader, we would all stop singing at the end of that verse, and the preacher would beg us one more time to make our hearts and our lives right with Jesus before it was too late. This would continue until we ran out of verses and started all over again. Pretty soon, on about the eighth or ninth stanza, the people who were sitting on those first few rows would have to move back to make room for all the convicted souls determined to change. Sometimes I cannot remember when I get to the grocery store what it was I came there for, but I will forever remember every word of every verse of "Just as I Am."

When a soul shuffled down that church aisle, it was an informed and educated decision based on true gospel sermons; it was a rational decision leading to a better life on earth; it was a spiritual decision banking on an eternal destiny; but let us never discount that it was also an emotional decision.

It's Charlie!

Bernice, rocking her baby and distanced from the crowd, could mostly hear only the song leader through the nursery speaker. It's the sound those with small children are used to, hearing every breath the song leader takes, and each occasional flat note, ". . . without one plea, but that Thy blood . . ." The view was composed of the backs of people's dresses and tweed suits through the glass as they stood, ". . . And that thou bid'st me come to thee . . ." As the other ladies watched another figure move toward the front, one of them said, "That looks like Charlie."

"Charlie? Charlie?" Bernice practically threw the baby off her lap into the floor, and suddenly became very interested in the glass window. "Where? Where?"

"Look over here," the answer came, "He walks like Charlie. What's Charlie wearing today?"

Oh, she couldn't even remember. She was stretching as far as she could to see the man that everyone else had seen a minute ago.

And just then—it must have been the end of the twelfth round, because the congregation began to settle back to the pews and funeral home fans—Bernice could see the top of a familiar sandy head. "It's Charlie," she whispered as if to God alone, and then, "It's Charlie!" in a scream so loud that all the babies began to cry. And then all the mothers

There is joy in the presence of the angels of God over one sinner who repents (Luke 15:10).

began to join them. It was an emotional moment because there is nothing tenderer to a heart than the knowledge that a lost sinner has left Satan's clutches and entered into the loving arms of the Father.

Bring Back the Tears of Joy!

A nursery full of young mothers wasn't the only scene of rejoicing the day that Charlie came to Christ. Luke lets us know there was some heavenly cheering for Charlie:

> Likewise, I say to you, there is joy in the presence of the angels of God over one sinner who repents (Luke 15:10).

Who's doing the rejoicing, the angels? Perhaps. That would certainly be a beautiful scene. But this verse doesn't say the angels are rejoicing, but that there is joy in their presence. Who is in the presence of the angels? There aren't a whole lot of beings we know of in answer to that question, are there? Our God is a rejoicing God, our God is an emotional God, and we are made in His image.

Moved to Tears

Just where does Luke 15:10 appear in Jesus' teachings? It is the opening line of my favorite story, the one about me. When the prodigal son had spent all and sat helpless envying pigs who were eating their fill, he came to himself and he came to the Father. What a sight he must have been, walking down that road in filthy rags and in need of shoes. It wasn't within his ability to make himself presentable to his Father. It never is. That's why the words of the song are so valuable: "Just as I am, without one plea."

In Acts 8, the Ethiopian went on his way rejoicing after becoming a Christian. In Acts 16, the jailer rejoiced for a night that had forever changed his life and those he loved.

There are those among us who dissuade the emotions so key in conversion. Particularly among the young and tender, there are

An Extra Helping

Celebrate the joy of coming to Christ with monthly spiritual baby showers. These should *not* be material in nature. Instead, wrap up notes, favorite Bible verses to lean on, advice, study helps, and bookmarks (see An Extra Helping, page 56) to nurture the new Christian in her walk. Above all, be present to grow a strengthening relationship. The only material gifts allowed are a new Bible signed by all and perhaps an inexpensive flashlight to represent her new light in Christ.

Serve clear punch to represent the cleansing that has occurred.

Clear Punch

(Makes 1 Gallon)

Dissolve 3 cups sugar in ¼ gallon warm water.
Add 1 teaspoon pineapple extract and 1 teaspoon orange extract.
(Use McCormick to keep from coloring punch.)
Add enough water to make a gallon.
The day before serving, add 2 tablespoons citric acid.

Rededication Memento

Alternately, for souls that are rededicating their lives:

Make a stash of "Just As I Am" stationery, and each time a soul responds to the gospel, rejoice with them with a little note.

"Just As I Am" Stationery

Shrink the page of the public domain hymn in your songbook.
Arrange 4 per page for printing.
Cut out, using shaped scissors to clip corners.
Glue to front of card made from folded cardstock. Accent corners with buttons.

If your congregation doesn't have one already, suggest a "love board" where cards can be addressed with name only and pinned to a cork board until discovered by the recipient.

often tears that accompany a decision to come to Christ, and to throw off the sin shackles.

In another book, I have stated that emotional decisions are not good ones. The context of that concerns snap decisions that do not consider the long run, but only what I feel like doing right now.

The decision to obey the gospel is different. It is one that examines the long, long run. Maybe there is too much emotion involved sometimes, but I fear far more that there is too little, especially among the "older and wiser." This is big. Why is it appropriate to cry at weddings and graduations and physical births, and to stare spiritual events stone cold in the face? This is a far greater occasion than the most remarkable of milestones, and yet I have heard some boast that the gospel message did not move them to tears as it did the weaker ones, as if that was a good thing.

At one glance from the Savior, Peter was convicted of his personal betrayal of Christ, and he had to leave the courtyard bursting into tears. "And the Lord turned and looked at Peter . . . So Peter went out and wept bitterly" (Luke 22:61–62).

Father, I have sinned against heaven and in your sight, and am no longer worthy to be called your son (Luke 15:21).

Don't Wait

I love Bible camp, and it's not because the bath house is 150 feet from the cabin; it's not because the mosquitoes are particularly prolific there; it's not because it is hotter than a sauna and more humid; and it's certainly not because I enjoy re-stringing the same string of beads a dozen times for the youngest camper in the craft quarters. It's because of a lot of things that have to do with Christian fellowship and time apart from the world. But more than anything else, it's the place where precious hearts are convicted that they don't want to be like that old world, but that they do want to do whatever it takes to live forever in this kind of fellowship.

Whatever happened to that the other fifty-one weeks of the year? Over and over I hear sincere broken young hearts repenting of their wrong during "the last year." If there's one thing I want to make them realize, it's that they don't have to wait until Bible camp. Sins can be—and are—washed away every day of the year. Every time we are gathered together as God's people, it's a golden opportunity to make that decision. What better place, what better environment to come with a broken heart to Christ? There in the presence of the people who care the most on this earth, and in the presence of the angels of heaven, sins are laid down and the cross is picked up. As Christ's blood streams down in unconstrained forgiveness, how can tears not stream down those overcome by that reality? And that's what "Just as I Am" is all about. Bring it back!

All twelve verses.

Soul Food

1. Is it possible to do too much persuading to influence someone's decision to obey the gospel? If so, at what point?

2. Were New Testament sermons heavy on persuasion? How do you think these sermons compare in emotional appeal to sermons today?

3. What influenced your decision to become a Christian? What emotions do you remember?

4. Besides the obvious rejoicing over the hopelessly lost being eternally saved, what other reasons to rejoice come about with a loved one being baptized into Christ?

5. Obeying the gospel is an intellectual, emotional, and spiritual decision. Which of these dimensions plays the biggest role, and how? How can we encourage or discourage this decision?

6. In Luke 15, there are two very different reactions to a sinner's restoration, that of the father and that of the older brother. What emotions did the Father show? What emotions did the older brother show? How does this story of a broken boy coming down the street parallel twenty-first century broken lives walking down the aisle and typical reactions to it?

7. The father saw the prodigal son barefooted and poorly clothed, so he put a robe on his shoulders, a ring on His finger, and shoes on His feet. How can we imitate the Father when a soul responds to the invitation today? What needs can we see—not necessarily physical—that we can immediately act upon to meet?

8. Find one or more sermons in scripture where the people were so emotional that they interrupted the sermon?

9. Within camps and other youth events, in addition to heartfelt conviction, there is also sometimes "drama" typical of the age group. When so much is on the line, how can we make sure we're using every opportunity to bring young people to Christ while also avoiding any tendency to act solely on emotions and peer influence? Is there a danger in this, and if so, what is it?

10. Is the invitation song found in scripture? Do a little research and find its origin. Is it a scriptural idea? What scriptures can you use to support this?

Were New Testament sermons heavy on persuasion? How do they compare today in emotional appeal?

A Favorite Piece

And speaking of weddings . . .

So is it just me, or are these things getting out of hand? My mom got married in a blue Sunday dress at her parents' house, and the most elaborate flaunting was that of tying perfectly good empty cans to a chrome bumper. What drew more attention were those shoe polish letters on the back windshield that read "Just Marred." It was an anonymous deed, but everybody knew that only Clarence could spell it that wrong.

Now the wedding thing is a production unequaled by the Grammies in sheer gaud, and mimicking the plot of *North by Northwest* in complexity. I thought it was crazy when I married that we had to stick each invitation in two envelopes for no good reason. Now you get an announcement that you're going to get an announcement later. The couples hire a professional photographer to take pictures of them looking like they're having fun in abandoned alleys and junk yards, and this is somehow related—and now required—to getting married. Who's paying for this, Warren Buffet?

The cost of a wedding dress is an arm, a leg, and half of your furniture hocked at the pawn shop. For what? Something cherished so genuinely that the brides are now having yet another photography session immediately after the wedding that's called, believe it or not, the "trash the dress" session.

A bowl of punch, a three-tiered cake, and a vase full of cashews. That's what wedding food used to be. Now it's hot wings and shrimp skewers, and get this: a picture of the bride *and* groom on each M&M. This is in a dimly lit reception hall, and I still couldn't see it with a magnifying glass and a flashlight.

I recently went to a wedding that had twenty-three brides-maids. Where'd she find all those people, and how much did she pay them to wear that? I've always found it a little unnatural to carry a bouquet around in front of you for an hour, and not actually do anything with it like put it in a vase or something. You just have to wonder is there a stain on that dress right there on the waistline? I've pulled that trick many times with a shopping bag at the mall.

I got married during the summer of eighty-nine, and it has been a wonderful marriage, but it came at the cost of a horrible wedding. I am really just now able to talk about it without either breaking down or throwing something at whoever brings it up.

It was kind of like that mice and men thing—the plans were well laid. But it ended up more resembling *A Comedy of Errors*. At first I felt like shooting for something sweet and old-fashioned. By the end, I just felt like shooting.

I had a seamstress make Victorian knickers for my husband's little brothers, who were then seven and nine. The outfits were adorable with pleated shirts and pronounced black bows. That's what they were meant to be, but keep in mind that seven and nine know nothing of adorable or Victorian. They know about karate and laser swords and two-point dunks, and they literally looked like they had been at the losing end of all three when the ceremony was over—sideways bowties, untucked shirttails, uneven pant lengths, and sagging, running stockings. (See the photo on page 116.)

They were the candle lighters, or they were supposed to be. The night before at rehearsal—a noun meaning a huge waste of time and your future in-laws' money—they each picked up the ornate, rented-for-a-large-sum-of-money, lighter/snuffer things, and gave them a thorough examination before con-cluding that they were a fancy strain of stick horses. Each did what any true Victorian cowboy would, immediately mounted them, and raced them up and down the aisles and through the pews.

The next day, neither the brass lighters nor the boy lighters were excited about the real assignment, and the brass ones refused to cooperate. The boy ones made a slight attempt. They marched down the aisle in grand style, but as Samuel—the seven one—got halfway down, his flame went out. He shrugged, and then raced back to the foyer as if the last one there was a full dozen rotten eggs, and his shoes must have had canastas attached to the heels. My dad relit the wick for him and sent him down the aisle again, but to no avail. This time Samuel breathed one of those audible whispers that Beethoven could have heard, even six feet under, "Well! It went out again!"

See, what I had envisioned was that my entire family, close friends, casual acquaintances, and electric meter reader would be brought to the precipice of tears at this point in the ceremony by the sheer beauty and significance of this solemn occasion. What actually happened was that I was already over the precipice back there, but not by beauty or significance, and the crowd filling the auditorium was having an unexpectedly grand time. Who would have thought that attending a wedding ceremony on a Saturday morning could be this much fun? There wasn't this much laughter at the *Hee-Haw* reunion.

This time my dad said, "I bet it doesn't go out again," and he gave the wick a stretch, suddenly giving meaning to the phrase "arm's length." The flame blazed with each step until we weren't sure we were at a wedding or a manhunt in an old Western.

And it wasn't just this, but the sound system malfunctioned, the ushers were more confused than a kindergarten class in a calculus club, and the slide show dedicated to the parents started abruptly while Mom and Dad were still in the bathroom.

We had planned to have the wedding early, so we could enjoy the rest of the day

There wasn't this much laughter at the *Hee-Haw* reunion.

in one another's adoration. What we didn't realize was that meant there was no prep time on the actual day, so we were getting haircuts at 3:00 in the morning the night before, and folding programs at 4:30. The first night of the honeymoon gave us what we had longed so deeply for—sleep!

Anniversaries are hard for me.

Hooray for revenge. My niece got married last summer, the first family wedding in twenty-four years. I secretly bought nose-and-glasses for all the groomsmen, and when the clock was supposed to chime at eight, it cuckooed instead.

"Hey, let's get the car," Caleb, brother of the bride said as he waved cans and tossed shoe polish to the rest of us, but he didn't think it through. Did it occur to him that he had been asked to drive the car from the church parking lot to a nearby mall, where the bride and groom would trade off the borrowed antique car for the real deal?

So here was Caleb rattling through town in a car brimming with balloons, tin cans dragging, and announcing "Just Married" on every square inch of window. And he was alone. Every driver on the road had to wonder what had happened to break up the marriage so soon.

Speaking of breaking up the marriage, it just wouldn't be a wedding if there wasn't a minor family rift. Someone wants to know why the second cousin was asked to serve punch when the first cousin wasn't even allowed to tie rice bags; Joyce got her invitation twelve days before Imogene; and everyone knows Freda bought a bedspread just to show up Chloe's dishtowels.

I suddenly understand why my mother kept telling me, "Now you know you can elope if you want to; just make sure and tell me first." Yes, she did.

But I didn't. There's something about proclaiming your irrevocable commitment to your one and only, in front of God and your dearest friends that gives focus to the rest of your life. But there's something about that other part—things I don't even have the strength to go into here, but which involve busted zippers, untimely classroom bells, and shattering hurricane lamps at gunshot decibels mid-ceremony—that make you second guess your mother's suggestion . . .

For as long as you both shall live.

Give Me that Old Time Religion

Give me that old time re - li - gion, Give me that old time re - li - gion,

Give me that old time re - li - gion, It's good e - nough for me.

WORDS & MUSIC: African American Spiritual

When asking whatever happened to fried chicken and the Joy bus and flowered polyester, I have to wonder what happened to some of those classic songs—*Pire in the Blood, Sweet Little Plums are Falling,* and *In Thy Field, I Would Yield Sickly, Brave, and True.* And if you ever tuned in a station on Sunday morning, you couldn't help but hear *Give Me That Old-Time Religion.* The altos whined like a pickup truck leaking power steering fluid, and every foot in the room just involuntarily started tapping—it was that kind of song.

Truth is, we were probably more enamored with the melody than the message. At second glance, what was the message? The previous chapters of this book reflected on things that are gradually slipping away from us, and as they quietly walk away, cautioned us to check their bags and make sure they're not smuggling something more important with them.

The remainder of the book examines just what we might be holding onto—holding tight as if it were a half-price coupon for the

Super Bowl, when in reality, it's ten percent off of last year's Toilet Bowl. Some traditions are not worth keeping because, as oversimplified as this may seem, they're only traditions.

Some traditions are, because they're more than that. The verses of the song alluded to, *Old Time Religion*, cover both.

Let's see.

It Was Good Enough for Mama . . .

(That's Irrelevant for Me)

So were metal hair rollers and rabbit ear antennas. But now that I know better, now that I know you can get a similar "do" with two minutes worth of curling iron, and you can pick up a full fifty times the number of channels without spending the better part of your life pulling the antennas in and out and wrapping aluminum foil around the top, now that I know—I've changed for the better.

Still, there's a great assurance to the lyric, and when it comes to material things, it's true. If it was good enough for Mama, then it should be good enough for me. It's hard to improve on Mama's life and the things she handed down to us, chicken and dressing recipes to be specific. Our lives are cluttered with fancier cars and more amazing kitchen gadgets, but when all is spread and spun, those material things haven't really improved our plight. At best they have given us convenience at 19.99

a pop, but at worst they have tugged our families in the direction of faster and finer until they have literally ripped us apart at the seams.

So the simple idea appeals to us: "If it was good enough for Mama, it's good enough for me." But when it comes to "old time religion," nothing could be more irrelevant. As dear as earthly parents may be to us, as drawn as we may be to their values, and as deeply indebted as we may be to their years of sacrifice because they cared more for us than any living being, one truth stands: Heavenly Father has to take precedence over earthly mother.

Any Other Gospel—Say It Again

I have seen the dearest of friends look scriptures square in the face, and shake their heads with, "That's what it says, but that's not what I've always been taught." The cognitive dissonance is crippling. It's why Paul repeated himself. This is so hard to swallow, and so crucial to your very soul, that he just had to say it twice:

> But even if we, or an angel from heaven, preach any other gospel to you than what we have preached to you, let him be accursed. As we have said before, so now I say again, if anyone preaches any other gospel to you than what you have received, let him be accursed (Galatians 1:8–9).

Even if it's Paul or Peter? Even if it's an angel from heaven? Even if it's Mama? Somehow Paul and Peter and the angel are easier to dismiss than Mama. I can't deny that it's possibly the hardest thing to grapple with for anyone who has experienced the love of a God-given mother who took that responsibility gravely and, without hesitation, would sacrifice her very life for her children. She couldn't steer us wrong, could she? I hope not, but for all the perfection wrapped up in

Heavenly Father has to take precedence over earthly mother.

the happy memories of home with that kind of mother, even Mama was a human being.

While Paul's message was so critical that it bore repeating, it's not the only time it happens in scripture. As with our own kids, when we want something to really sink in, we say it more than once.

I remember a high school friend of mine whose mother wanted to make certain she had covered all the bases. "Barbara, did I ever tell you," her tone was sober, "to line the public toilet seats with paper before you sit on them?" Only probably a thousand times. But that's how it is with parents. There are things we *know* we've said before, but we're so concerned that our kids somehow missed them, that those are the things we find ourselves repeating.

Not everyone who says to Me, "Lord, Lord," shall enter the kingdom of heaven, but he who does the will of My Father in heaven (Matthew 7:21).

That Seems Right

God is the ultimate Parent. There are things He just knows we're going to miss the first time, and they are so eternally important that He chooses to repeat them. Galatians 1:8–9 is one of them, but here's another which happens to be very similar: "There is a way that seems right to a man, but its end is the way of death" (Proverbs 14:12). But look at Proverbs 16:25: "There is a way that seems right to a man, but its end is the way of death."

Wait! You said that already. Yes, He did—verbatim! Why is it so important that God Almighty had to repeat Himself? Because our soul can be misled eternally if we miss this warning. It can seem like the right thing—the right way to a man or a woman or even Mama, but the end is disastrous.

Where is our allegiance? Quite frankly, because frankness is often what we really need, Jesus said, "He who loves father or mother more than Me is not worthy of Me" (Matthew 10:37). Are we worthy of Jesus?

Get It Right

My mother was a school teacher, so when I struggled with some lessons in the fourth grade, my math teacher said, "Celine, why don't you see if your mother can help you with this?" The answer I gave was a frank one as well, and the teacher couldn't get down the hall fast enough to tell my mother. "I think that's the problem," I said, "She's been helping me."

My mother was giving me the help that seemed right. She was a teacher, loved education, and probably cared more about my schooling than anyone else. Yet the conclusions she was leading me to, or at least the ones I thought she was leading me to, didn't line up with the standard—the math book. Unless and until I myself arrived at the proper understanding of the concrete truths in that book, failure was in store.

Could it be that my mother wanted that failure for me, so long as I could lean on the help she had given me? Of course not. She

An Extra Helping

Purchase an antique math book and a Bible with a worn cover, and tie them together with an attractive ribbon (or one of Mama's apron strings). Place them on an end table or a shelf leaned up against a favorite accent piece. When people (those who live under your roof and guests) notice or ask about it, it gives you an opportunity to explain the relationship of the two books because they both hold concrete truths, and there is an importance in getting it exactly like the book teaches.

wanted me to get it right! She wanted me to get it exactly like the book said. Good mamas always do.

In studying the Bible with your children, haven't you said, "It doesn't matter what I think or what you think but what God says"? Don't we hope in our heart of hearts that our children will always choose God's directive over ours, if there is ever a conflict of the two?

If ever in our personal study of God's Word, we find a truth that Mama missed, is it a dishonor to her if we internalize and obey it? I'd say it's a dishonor to her if we don't. It's what she wanted, for her child to come to the understanding of the concrete truths exactly as the book teaches. She wants me to get it right!

Leave Them More than a Legacy

But now one more thought, and this one's for the mamas. Let's make sure when we leave this world that we don't leave our children with this dilemma. It goes without saying that we want our lives to be an example for them, but beyond that, we want to hold up God's Word in our homes with the highest of respect. Anytime they ask a moral or doctrinal question, the answer does not begin with, "Well, I've always been taught,"; "The preacher says . . . "; "We believe . . . ", but the answer always begins with, "Let's see what the Bible says." With that foundation, children will always be led to the right answer, years and generations after Mama can no longer answer those questions for them.

What is good enough? "It is enough for a disciple that he be like his teacher" (Matthew 10:25). And I think my mama would have agreed.

Wouldn't yours?

"Let's see what the Bible says." With that foundation, children will always be led to the right answer, generations after Mama.

Observe and obey all these words which I command you, that it may go well with you and your children after you forever, when you do what is good and right in the sight of the Lord your God.
—Deuteronomy 12:28

Soul Food

1. Make a list of things that were good enough for Mama that you'd hate to have to settle for now.

2. Besides Galatians 1:8–9; Proverbs 14:12; and 16:25; list some other places in scripture where God repeats the same thing. In what way are these critical?

3. What reminder did your earthly parents give you over and over again? Why was it so important to them?

4. What idea, if any, did you grow up accepting one way, but upon examining scripture, are clearly convinced of a different understanding?

A Favorite Piece

And speaking of 19.99 a pop . . .

Who thinks of these things? I speak of the Dream-gadget, the Snuggle-uppie, the Hair-doozie, and other amazing things which aren't in the dictionary, but which cost 19.95. It's as if they have a window on my life, and know the issues that keep me awake at night, and which fit into the following categories:

I was pretty content with the abs I have until I realized that with a six-second workout, my abs could be amazing, but only if I was willing to fork over the 19.95. It's true. With a six-second workout, I really can have amazing abs. People whisper about my abs as I walk by at the grocery store. It sounds like the first person says, "Look at those pitiful abs." But I know the second one says, "That's amazing."

Other people don't have as much luck. I have a friend who ordered a "gut buster" a few years ago, but so far, hers hasn't busted.

How will the kids go to college unless I secure their future? 19.95 today could actually turn into more for my financial future tomorrow (maybe even 19.96) turning my otherwise dull home into a beautiful museum of collectible fine art pieces that come in the form of plates, paperweights, and Barry Manilow.

Valuable coins which depict historical events in vivid color amaze my friends, but don't do much at the laundromat. So now they've decided to call it what it is. I recently saw an ad for "America's obsolete coin collection." I'm serious; that's really what they call it. Just thinking out loud, but does it make sense to spend 19.95 in working, usable currency for a collection of coins which they admit in their advertising is obsolete? Who's backing this, Bernie Madoff?

I decide to hold on to the real currency, but the offers come faster and stronger.

I was still pondering the wearable blanket idea, trying to get past the idea that seven out of ten Americans are missing that they could just put on their robe backwards. Before I could fully resolve that, I was broadsided with a deeper issue. There it was on the screen. They were doing this to dogs now.

If the humans want to lay around reading a good book and looking like Yoda, and they are fully consenting adults, who am I to stop them? But it's a little unfair to get the dogs involved. Dogs aren't really good with fashion, by nature. They're kind of like Job: naked they came, and naked they will return. So if they're going to parade around in clothes, they're kind of at your mercy concerning what's a good sweater and what doesn't, you know, make them look fat. Point blank: they have no idea how ridiculous they look in the blanket with arms. That's why they're the only ones who don't laugh at you in yours. Isn't it cruelty to dress them that way, and when will PETA step up and get involved?

Some of the pet offers are more desirable. Imagine my excitement when I found out about the new cat emery board. This has been a constant source of conflict in our home. Every time I sit down to file my nails, the cat has taken my emery board to her vanity and is giving herself a manicure. No more sharing. Life is easy, especially considering that if I order now, I can get not one, but two of these things. Even the neighbor's cat can join in the fun. We can have makeover parties.

But wait! There's more. Come to find out if you call toll-free this very minute, you get a cute kitty toy and a packet of catnip. This conjures images of totally high kitties running around with fresh manicures, and I'm thinking my cat could be on *Access Hollywood*.

I guess she'll be pretty embarrassed by the dog in the backward housecoat chasing his tail and drinking out of the toilet. That's where the sonic dog saber comes in handy. Here's how it works on the commercial. When your dog does something annoying like "chew on

> I guess she'll be pretty embarrassed by the dog in the backward housecoat chasing his tail and drinking out of the toilet.

your grandmother's purse" or "stand in front of the TV during final Jeopardy," you just pick up the device and point it at him, and he immediately turns into one of those dogs that I've heard about who actually cooperates with his owner.

Give me that thing. Does it work on people? I have always wanted to have that power.

"Clean out the dishwasher!" I point with the sonic pointer.

"Stop snoring." (*Point.*)

"Don't eat that last brownie." (*Point.*)

I've often been plagued by the cumbersome job of loading and unloading my recliner out of the minivan. Then my friend Stan recommended the anywhere chair for only—you guessed it; I must admit this came in handy on the escalator, and again at the ensuing court hearing.

Another concern has been keeping my children occupied with healthy activities. After a while they get bored with opening the piano and launching things from the internal keys. And we all know that dropping obsolete coins into the duct work can only entertain them for so long.

That's when my friends told me about the aqua doodle. This has passed hours of time when my daughter could have been doing something less exciting like changing the fish tank which is now turning into its own aqua doodle.

Call me crazy but I'm just a little apprehensive about paying 19.95 for something with sham in its title. Wow! I'm also a little apprehensive about the purpose of some of these things. They're supposed to make life better, right? No more tossing and turning at night. No more unsightly furniture tears. Say goodbye to scratches and paint a room in less than an hour. But now we have this— something they're calling atomic putty. What? Now if you can't get the stain out, just blow the thing up? Does homeland security know?

> Dropping obsolete coins into the duct work can only entertain them for so long.

But all in all, it's a vote for good old American ingenuity, even if the product names sound slightly like a Pokémon rerun. Where else can you get something that dices, slices, and mops up orange juice for under twenty bucks? Besides, 19.95 doesn't sound so bad when I'm informed that I would have to pay seventy, ninety, even one hundred dollars to get this product in a store. And yet, get this—it's not available in *any* store!

Why would anybody pay a hundred dollars for something in a store that doesn't even sell it?

One day I'm going to sit in my anywhere chair in my snuggle-uppie and figure all this out, but for now, more urgent matters. I think I hear my cat using my best nail clippers.

It Was Good for the Hebrew Children . . .

(But It's Better for Me)

So was this: "And he shall offer from it all its fat. The fat tail and the fat that covers the entrails" (Leviticus 7:3). It's just one random command from all the ones that I should give thanks about every day—thanks that they're no longer binding!

There's no doubt it was good for the Hebrew children. It has always been good for God's people. Goshen was always the best part of Egypt because that's where God's people were. Scripture tells us in Exodus 8 that the grievous swarm of flies was so severe that it destroyed the land. But in Goshen I imagine no one even asked where the fly swatter was. It was good for the Hebrew children.

Then and Now

When they got hungry, food fell from the sky. When they got thirsty, water flowed out of a rock. When they came to a seeming impasse, an entire sea split open in the middle, and they walked right through it. It was good for the Hebrew children.

When the Hebrews were finally preparing to cross the Jordan and conquer Canaan, God gave them a heads up on what would happen. "Every place that the sole of your foot shall tread upon, that have I given unto you, as I said to Moses" (Joshua 1:3). When God blesses, He's thorough. It wasn't just a piece of cake; it was three layers with caramel icing. It was good for the Hebrew children.

But it's better for me—the New Testament book of Hebrews is dedicated to telling us why. It was written to the nation that understood how great God's provision was for the Hebrew children, who had a bloodline that went all the way back to the wilderness and beyond. They got that God was good to their nation, and I think if they had known the tune back then, they would have sung out the loudest, "It was good for the Hebrew children, and it's good enough for me."

The writer of Hebrews affirms, yes, it was good for the Hebrew children, but that was then; this is now! He wastes no time in getting to point number one in the first two verses.

> God, who at various times and in various ways spoke in time past to the fathers by the prophets, has in these last days spoken to us by His Son, whom He has appointed heir of all things, through whom also He made the worlds (Hebrews 1:1–2).

We Have a Better Messenger

God has always wanted men to respect His messengers. Korah, Dathan, and Abiram didn't, and on top of their contempt for Moses, when they were summoned, they simply said, "We will not come up!" (Numbers 16:12, 14).

This was not followed by a lengthy debate on prophetical authority. It was followed by, "Get away from the tents of Korah, Dathan, and Abiram" (Numbers 16:24). You know the rest of the story.

Fast forward to Hebrews 2.

Therefore we must give the more earnest heed to the things we have heard, lest we drift away. For if the word spoken through angels proved steadfast, and every transgression and disobedience received a just reward, how shall we escape if we neglect so great a salvation, which at the first began to be spoken by the Lord, and was confirmed to us by those who heard Him? (Hebrews 2:1–3).

Jesus is a better messenger, and with better blessings comes greater responsibility. The better messenger has summoned us, "Go into all the world and preach the gospel to every creature" (Mark 16:15). He's summoned us, "Whoever compels you to go one mile, go with him two" (Matthew 5:41). In telling of the Samaritan wounds-wrapper who converted his donkey to an ambulance, he summoned us to "go and do likewise" (Luke 10:37). What message are we sending back? Is it ever, "We will not go up"? We ought to do better.

We Have Better Promises

What would you do to get a great inheritance? In 1926 Charles Van Millar's will revealed that his estate would be converted to cash and given to the woman who could give birth to the most children within a ten-year period. At the rate I was going in my younger years, I could have been a contender. Turns out, the inheritance was split between three women who had nine children each. I guess it's true that nothing can be gained without hard labor. Or can it?

As strange as the circumstances are, Millar, even after death, was true to his promise. God is truer, and as the Hebrew children were suffering under Egyptian tyrants and slave masters, He made a

With better blessings comes greater responsibility.

promise: "I have said I will bring you up out of the affliction of Egypt to the land of the Canaanites and the Hittites and the Amorites and the Perizzites and the Hivites and the Jebusites, to a land flowing with milk and honey" (Exodus 3:17). He was as good as His word. He still is.

We Have a Better Inheritance

The difference is that the promise is even better. The inheritance is even greater. Not one of those Hebrew children who triumphantly crossed the Jordan and conquered the Promised Land is enjoying it today. Oh, they drank the milk and sopped the honey, but all good things must come to an end. Under that law.

An Extra Helping

Here are two ways to keep your perspective where it needs to be all year by using 12 "betters" from Hebrews.

1. *"Better" Family Calendar.* Get with 11 family members (physical or spiritual) and have them each electronically submit a photograph to you of a sentimental spot or sentimental items that are weathered with age. (Physical treasure perish, but spiritual ones are better!) Using the following list, add different text to each one, submit to an online calendar-maker, and share the cost.

   • A better name (1:4)—This would go well with a rusted sign from a favorite downtown spot frequented in childhood.

   • Better things (6:9)—Childhood tangibles

   • A better hope (7:19)

   • A better testament (7:22 KJV)

   • A better covenant (8:6)

   • Better promises (8:6)

How about a land where it doesn't come to an end? God promises us, under His new and better law, an inheritance that is incorruptible (1 Peter 1:4). You can't get that here, or from anyone else. Money just doesn't hold its value. I was watching an episode of the *Andy Griffith Show* this week and a man rented a hotel room for an entire night for a dollar and twenty-five cents. How many seconds of lodging could that get you now?

I'm crazy about dilapidated old buildings. I don't know why but I think it's because I envision the stories they can tell. I see proud new home owners walking around in Victorian clothing, little boys shooting shiny marbles on the back porch, parlors full of laughter and singing, and pianos being pounded. Look at the structure

- Better sacrifices (9:23) — Old aprons or worn shoes could symbolize "sacrifice" here.
- Better possession (10:34 ESV)
- A better country (11:16)
- A better resurrection (11:35)
- Something better (11:40)
- A better word (12:24 ESV)

2. *"Better" Refrigerator Reminders.* Cut out the word *better* from a magazine, and glue to a magnetic strip (purchased in a roll from the craft department). Coat with Mod Podge or a spray finish. This stays up on your fridge all year.

Now do the same with the other words, and on the first of each month, change the word to remind you of yet another way that the Christian life is better than any other. Some words may be harder to find in magazines than others, so you may have to cut out individual letters in fun colors and fonts.

now. Where are the happy inhabitants? The ceilings are sagging, the windows are broken, and weeds shoot up through the parlor floor. It could use a coat of paint! The sad truth: it's corrupted, and it will happen to the best of the brick mansions given enough time. I watched on television as a wrecking ball crashed through the house that was the center of the classic novel, *The Great Gatsby,* and I remember screaming, "Noooooo!" from my living room.

And then I kicked myself and told myself to get over it because that's not my house. I have an inheritance that's incorruptible. I have a greater promise.

I have an inheritance that's undefiled. The Hebrew children had a great inheritance, but it was quickly defiled. In Joshua 6 the walls of Jericho fell down, and the city was theirs for the taking. In the very first verse of Joshua 7 the inheritance was defiled. Sin messed up the inheritance for the Hebrew children before they could say "Chapter 7." Sin still messes up the inheritance. But here's the difference. Sin can rob us of the inheritance only when it is our sin, and that's when it's this side of the Jordan.

It can interfere with our claiming the prize, but if we access God's grace and fix our eyes on the inheritance, nothing is going to spoil it. It's a better inheritance—it's undefiled. It's a better promise which gives us the next thing.

We Have a Better Hope

The Israelites named in Hebrews 11 lived their lives in hope of attaining the prize—that inheritance. There was also some knowledge of a heavenly inheritance. It's where Enoch was; David longed to be with his infant son again there; and verses 13 through 16 clearly teach that those faith icons who were pilgrims here, were focused there. However, the Way (John 14:6) had not yet appeared. Hebrews 12:2 calls Jesus the Finisher. They had a hope, but now that the Finisher has come, and the Way has connected broken man to perfect God, our hope is sure. It's better.

When you're given a puzzle in a box, you know that one day it can become a beautiful picture. If it has a thousand pieces, and it's still in the shrink wrap when you get it, you have a hope of what it will become. But then, when you have almost all the pieces connected, and you look at the box and see the last three pieces and where they will fit, you have a surer hope. It's as good as finished.

Looking unto Jesus, the author and finisher of our faith (Hebrews 12:2).

We Have a Better Covenant

To start with, the seal of the old covenant was circumcision. I guess it's one way to see who's seriously committed. But another thing—the old covenant was more difficult to know and keep. There were stipulations concerning sacrifices regarding putting blood on the horns, and what exactly to do with the caul and the liver and the inward parts. It varied according to whether it was a sin offering or a peace offering, and exactly who was doing the sinning and the offering.

Not only did laws apply to meats which were classified as clean or unclean based on hoof-splits and cud-chewing, but it further depended on what either the meat or the eater had touched recently. Present day school nurses who nit-pick schoolchildren's hair for lice have nothing on Levitical priests, who based their diagnoses of leprosy on whether head sores were reddish, whitish, or freckled. When you dig into Leviticus, the law was stringent; it was complicated. It was good because it came from the Best, and it is what set the Hebrew children far above the heathen in cleanliness, health, and wellbeing, both physically and spiritually. It was good for the Hebrew children. But it gets better.

"A new commandment I give to you," Jesus said in John 13:34, "that you love one another; as I have loved you." Better. At least five times Jesus said in the Sermon on the Mount, "You have heard that it has been said," and each time it's followed with, "But I say to you . . . "Stipulations concerning murder and manslaughter and cities of refuge and judgment by a city's elders are exchanged for the simpler and more beautiful command not to harbor anger without cause (Matthew 5:21–22). Better. Adultery laws which had carried varying sentences and employed the earliest of lie detectors (Numbers 5) were now taken care of with the sensible command not to look around and not to lust within (Matthew 5:27–28). Better. The complications of divorce writings and Old Testament polygamy were solved with one solid verse on the permanence of the husband-wife relationship and one obvious exception (Matthew 5:31–32). Better. The old rules concerning the conditions for swearing were twisted and abused, but the new deal was simply to let your word be good, and there would be no need for swearing (Matthew 5:33–37). Getting even was traded for non-retaliation (Matthew 5:38–39). Loving your neighbor was upgraded to loving your enemy (Matthew 5:43–44). Better, better, better!

The old covenant was for the Hebrew children, but God's point from the beginning in separating a people through this covenant was to eventually bless all nations with that lineage through Jesus Christ. Because of that, the new covenant is for my race too, and, in fact, it's for me personally. It's better.

Finally, the old covenant required a human link to access God. Any time humans are involved in an access road, expect occasional road bumps and potholes. Aaron had the "earrings spontaneously forming cows" problem, Eli had to have had the most dysfunctional family around, and God was so fed

Aaron had the "earrings spontaneously forming cows" problem, up with the priests by the time we get to the book of Malachi that He wouldn't accept their offerings. Well, that road crew was forced into retirement. We have a God-link to God now.

I'm sitting in a fast food establishment under a TV tuned to CNN as I write this, and as you can imagine, it has been story after story of governments, agreements, constitutions tainted with human errors at best, and human corruption at worst.

Not so with my heavenly agreement. It's a covenant that bypasses the human hierarchy and connects me directly with inerrant God, and that's just plain better.

> We do not have a High Priest who cannot sympathize with our weaknesses, but was in all *points* tempted as *we are*, *yet* without sin (Hebrews 4:15).

We Have a Better Resurrection

Hebrews 11:35 alludes to a couple of the few instances recorded in scripture where, through God's amazing power, the dead were actually brought back to life. That doesn't happen any more. I imagine everyone reading this has had that feeling at least once. It's that gnawing sick daze, and hoping you will wake up and it won't really be true, that somehow the person you love will really still be alive. But you and I know—you don't wake up from that reality. You just trust in a God that, in a way we'll never understand, takes you by the hand and gets you through it.

Imagine the joy that took place on those occasions in scripture where God really did back up and reverse the death event. It happened in 1 Kings 17 when a widow's only son became sick and tragically died. She did what any of us would probably do; she blamed the only person she could; the only one who was there, calling him the man of God, but finding no comfort in it. She was destitute and desperate, until Elijah took the dead boy, laid him on his own bed, and pled with God to "let this child's soul come back to him" (1 Kings 17:21).

It happened in 2 Kings 4 when a mother held her sick little boy in her lap until noon, helpless, until at last the child died. But later that same dark, dreadful day turned into the most joyous occasion of a lifetime. Never before or again was there such celebration over a sneeze.

Women received their dead raised to life again. And others were tortured, not accepting deliverance, that they might obtain a better resurrection (Hebrews 11:35).

The same verse in Hebrews that mentions these remarkable events, says that others "were tortured, not accepting deliverance, that they might obtain a better resurrection." Better? What could possibly be better than what happened on these two occasions?

As New Testament Christians, our resurrection far surpasses those Old Testament ones. For starters, it's a permanent resurrection. I can't wrap my finite mind around the infinite, but there is no end to that life when we are resurrected.

Second, it's a resurrection that will reunite us with every saved or safe—in the case of children—person that we have struggled to let go of, with tears and sleepless nights. I will forever be with the person who rocked me through midnight fevers, the one who hiked the mountains with me in the fall, and the college friend who loved laughing more than anything. I'll be with Paul, who has pulled me through uncertain times, and James, who has nudged me back where I needed to be.

It's a better resurrection because it will be untainted with the problems of this life. The little boys who were resurrected in the Old Testament were in for hardships—physical pain, emotional pain, temptation, and sin and its ugly consequences. Not so for us—this resurrection exempts all that.

But far above these reasons, as if any one of them is not enough, these boys awoke to see human faces. Oh, God was there, and He is here with each of us always, but then "we shall be like him, for we shall see him as He is" (1 John 3:2). This crescendos the "better" symphony of Hebrews. What more could be imagined or created to surpass this euphoria?

All Sons of God

I repeatedly hear some Christians say if they had lived in Old Testament times, it would be easier to be faithful because of all the direct revelations and amazing miracles. Did they really have it easier? Don't give yourself a pass because you don't live in the age of talking donkeys and floating fingers writing on walls. You want to have a direct line to God, or do you want a priest to do it for you? You want to get into what animals to sacrifice and when and how much blood to sprinkle in order to appease God for your sins, or do you want to be baptized into Christ and once and for all allow His blood to completely forgive, cleanse, and give you a clean slate?

To make a pitiful word picture, do you want to drive around on the temporary spare, or do you want a new tire? Oh, the temporary spare is important. It gets us off the side of the road and moving in the right direction until we can get the real thing. I'm thankful for it! But it's temporary.

We didn't come to the concert for the warm-up band.

> Therefore the law was our tutor to bring us to Christ, that we might be justified by faith. But after faith has come, we are no longer under

Don't give yourself a pass because you don't live in the age of talking donkeys and floating fingers writing on walls.

a tutor. For you are all sons of God through faith in Christ Jesus
(Galatians 3:24–26).

It just doesn't get any better than that.

> *Therefore, since we are receiving a kingdom which cannot*
> *be shaken, let us have grace, by which we may serve*
> *God acceptably with reverence and godly fear.*
> —Hebrews 12:28

Soul Food

1. What disastrous consequences, other than those to Korah, Dathan, and Abiram, came to Old Testament men or women who disregarded God's commands?

2. Only some of the "betters" of Hebrews are mentioned in this chapter. What are the others? Which "better" do you personally treasure the most? Why?

3. Are a better inheritance, a better promise, a better hope, and a better resurrection all virtually the same thing, or are they distinctively different things? Explain your answer.

4. In your life, what thing have you had a hope for, and then as time and events changed, that hope became surer?

5. Review the events of Joshua 7 when an inheritance was quickly defiled. In what ways did the sin of one man impact an entire nation? How far reaching do you think the consequences may have been?

6. Check several newspaper or internet news source this week. Make a note any time you see sin interfering with the joys promised by earthly wealth.

7. In Matthew 5, notice each time Jesus says, "A new commandment I give unto you." Were these radical in that culture? Are these radical in our culture? Are these new "principle" commandments easier or harder to accept than the "letter" commandments?

8. A couple of complicated Leviticus commands are given which are no longer binding. Find a command in either Leviticus or Numbers which makes you particularly glad you are not living under that law.

A Favorite Piece

And speaking of swarms of flies and fly swatters . . .

Life on the front porch might be a little more at ease without them, but it wouldn't be half as hilarious. How is it that a tiny flying insect with a miniscule sliver of a stinger can create chaos that sounds like Bonnie and Clyde have made a comeback? My mother used to add life to every picnic by getting stung by a little thing that made her swell like a big thing. Our favorite was when the bee planned an ambush under an ice cube in her drink, and attacked her tongue on the way down.

We showed up to the emergency room (because we were afraid the swelling might obstruct air passages) barely able to communicate the details for laughing so hard. Even though Mama's tongue was swelled markedly, don't think for a minute something that insignificant could keep her from talking. It could, however, keep her from talking in any kind of normal fashion. So that each time on the drive there that she said, "Thlow down" or "Watch the thtop thign!" we bellowed louder than the time before. By the time she said, "Where'th my purth?" when asked for an insurance card, we had lost our breath and could answer only in silent laughter coming from mouths mounted to necks cocked back in surrender.

See, I have seriously heard people ask why God would create flies and bees and other winged things, and though I don't pretend to have the key to God's wisdom, I do know that life sure would be missing some highlights without them. Highlights like the time my sister spotted a moth flying around the light fixture in the dining room over our supper. She nervously emitted a couple of short yelps, trying to avoid getting in trouble at the table, before the thing began to descend, and she gave up all hope of any etiquette. This is when she opened her mouth and let it all out, and let it all in as well. What greater place for a moth to explore than a giant opening right there at the table?

I'm not sure why children are so intrinsically scared of bugs, but it has made for interesting camp-outs and road trips, and has interfered with many a good night's sleep. I remember a trip to Jackson, Mississippi, to see the state capitol where I feel that most of the tourists thought they were getting to see not only the capitol, but hear the capital murder as my daughter screamed violently at the thought of the housefly coming within ten feet of her.

The Deep South is full of those pests. We hang zip-lock bags full of water in the kitchen windows to keep them away. I have no idea what that plan is. Are flies afraid of bags of water? Are flies afraid of people who would be loopy enough to hang bags of water in their kitchens?

> She nervously emitted a couple of short yelps, trying to avoid getting in trouble at the table.

142

But it's not just flies; mosquitoes definitely favor the Mississippi region when it comes to vacationing. The bleachers at the little league field come alive as people wave their arms in sync at dusk. It might be mistaken for team spirit, and much resembles the motion in the movie *Angels in the Outfield*, but make no mistake, it's just an empty hope that not as many mosquitoes can hit a moving target.

When we moved out of Mississippi, we had a group of movers drive eight hours to help us load boxes onto the U-Haul. Their intentions were noble, but as soon as dusk hit, five grown men came running in the front door clawing their legs with both hands, defeated by something you could squish with a raisin.

> Five grown men came running in the front door clawing their legs with both hands, defeated by something you could squish with a raisin.

And speaking of squishing, who hasn't been faced with the dilemma of what to grab when your eight-legged enemy is defying you to hit him? You reach for a book without taking your eyes off the villain, and the best you can come up with is a Bible or an autographed copy of a rare edition, so you know you've got to resort to the shoes. This is the main reason I dislike high heels. They are not versatile enough to serve the dual purpose for which shoes were intended. So my weapons have consisted of cereal boxes, teething rings, teddy bears, and hair spray bottles, which explains why the bathroom mirror is cracked and the cabinet door won't shut all the way to this day. And why most of our library inventory has matching brown splotches.

I heard some kind of crashing commotion downstairs about midnight when my son had a friend over. It really didn't faze me, as I would be more disturbed if there were not signs of barbaric activity down there. The next morning I found an antique plate on the table, which had previously hung on the wall, pieced together like a factory-seconds jigsaw puzzle. There was a note:

> I was trying to kill a fly.
> Im sincerely sorry.
> Nathan

Now, just thinking out loud here, but isn't it kind of likely that given another two seconds, the fly might have relocated to a spot, maybe less glass and less antique?

At least flies and wasps (sprayed by Lysol) do the decent thing: die when killed, and stay dead. Ants are not so cooperative. You can squish them, drown them, decapitate them, dissect them, suffocate them with a plethora of poisons—herbal, natural, organic, and chemically explosive and illegal—and within five minutes, you're staring at a robust specimen strutting around with a set of snacks twenty times his body weight. "Hey, aren't you the same guy I just . . . ?" It's not enough that he shows up again, but he brings all his relatives, on both sides, with him.

Face it! Insects are annoying, but if you ever doubt that they liven up the party just a little bit, then you need to watch a good round of *Fire Ants at the Wedding Reception.*

It Was Good for
Paul and Silas
(And That's Encouraging to Me)

It sure was, and whenever I need an extra dose of encouragement, I think about Paul and Silas. I think that's kind of neat that two people that I have never met in person, and that have been dead and gone longer than kudzu has been growing on old cars, can encourage me more than most people who are alive and making mortgage payments. It's just that way with God's Word. Its encouragement spans the centuries.

Stuck in a Leg Lift

Here were Paul and Silas in Acts 16, in far worse circumstances than I was when I was lost in the city of Manila on a mission trip, or when I was crammed up in a cheap motel that I couldn't even afford because my borrowed van had broken down on the side of the road, again, or when I stood beside an emergency room bed while they ran a tube through my one-year-old son's neck and pumped charcoal into his stomach. You can add your miseries to the list—all those times we have screamed "Why me?" or felt like it.

You don't hear any *why me*'s from Paul and Silas, though their circumstances were far more extreme. If someone had committed a heinous crime in those days, you might think they would reap one of several punishments. Perhaps they would be beaten with stripes. It was called that for a reason. You didn't walk away from a Roman beating without everyone you met knowing it. The whips literally tore into your skin until you were striped. And remember, the Roman stripe sentence had no limit; you could only pray your beater's arms got tired.

Perhaps such offenders would be locked away in this kind of prison:

> With few exceptions, prisons in the Roman period were dark, disease-ridden, and overcrowded places. It was common for prisoners to die in custody, either from disease or starvation, brutal torture, execution, or suicide. Imprisonment is commonly described by ancient authors as a fate worse than death; even the thought of it was appalling (Marshall 6).

Or maybe they would be subjected to the miserable stocks fastened to their ankles. We are probably most familiar with medieval stocks that we sometimes see on tours of antiquity. These would be bad enough. How would you like to be stuck in a leg-lift six to twelve inches off the ground for hours—even days? Certain of my body parts are getting sore just thinking about it. And there is no exercise mat here; not even plush carpet. How about a dirt floor in the dark at best, and more probable an uneven stone one? However, in Roman

How would you like to be stuck in a leg-lift six to twelve inches off the ground for hours—even days?

times the stocks were probably even more primitive; huge unfinished bulks of wood more like logs which contorted the legs in unnatural positions. Because both feet were put in separate, difficult to move, rough-wood beams, a person's body was desperate to find any tolerable position.

> These men, being Jews, exceedingly trouble our city (Acts 16:20).

The Darkest Hour

The loom of any of these three punishments would keep me going the speed limit on a two-lane road, but Paul and Silas got all three. And the bad deal was, they hadn't done a thing wrong. In fact, they had done a thing right. They had healed a girl possessed by a spirit, and because she had been a Jackson Square-type freak show, her producers were just a little upset by their sudden income loss. So they did what any low-down, revenge-seeking, money-serving rascals would do—they just made up lies that Paul and Silas were causing trouble in the city, and teaching people to do illegal things (Acts 16:17–21).

That's a sickening feeling—to know you haven't done anything wrong, and to be accused of it: defriended, betrayed, isolated—in the words of a *Sesame Street* monster—sad, sad, sad. It also draws you closer to God: He and you are the only ones who know of a certainty the truth.

That's how it worked for Paul and Silas. They were drawn closer to God "at midnight." It's the darkest hour. They got there through false accusation, but there are a lot of ways to get there. Some of them are faster than others. Some take twists and painful turns on the way, and some of them just plop you there hard when you're going along fat, dumb, and happy. Whatever the route, you find yourself at midnight, the darkest hour, and you start doing what Paul and Silas were doing in a way that only midnight brings.

> But at midnight Paul and Silas were praying and singing hymns to God, and the prisoners were listening (Acts 16:25).

Fervent Praying and Sustaining Singing

"Paul and Silas were praying." Even the disobedient and rebellious pray at midnight, but it's the greatest comfort to know that "the effective, fervent prayer of a righteous man avails much" (James 5:16). I get the idea that this fit the criteria, that it was pretty fervent. I get the feeling they were doing some serious one-on-One. I can't prove it, but the prayer probably wasn't composed of the standards: "Guide, guard, and direct us until we meet again"; "Be with the sick of our number"; and "Go with us to our respective places." Those are good sentiments when they stream from the conscience (and not the unconscious), but fervency is going to unfold in cries for help specific to the crisis.

". . . And singing hymns to God." Are you serious? W. C. Handy was not the father of the blues, as we have been told? In jail, in writhing discomfort, in pain, wrongly accused and arrested, we might say they were ripe for the blues. They were more than ripe: they were fallen off and squishy. But what they did was amazing; they broke out in song. And it wasn't the Roman version of *Rocky Top* or *Free Bird*. If so, it would have been useless, and I don't think they would have bothered. But these were hymns to God. It's a unique communication that only God's own know. He instilled in us a voice for song, and then told us to use it. What is it about a song that moves us, that sustains us, that draws us so close to our Father? It closes out the stocks that bind us and the wounds that hurt us and places us into caring arms that soothe us.

> The earth closed over them, and they perished from among the assembly (Numbers 16:33).

Futility to Faith

Take a look at Psalms. Remember, while we read them as poetry and prose, each psalm was just that—it was a song. And at times Beale Street would look like Disneyland when lined up against the backdrop of these original blues singer/psalm-writers' circumstances. These songs are filled with tears, trouble, intense feelings of rock bottom despair, but in almost all of them, somewhere along the way, the psalmist either gradually or abruptly shifts from futility to faith, and there is a glorious triumph that almost comes through in crescendo as you read. Notice:

> The pangs of death surrounded me, and the floods of ungodliness made me afraid. The sorrows of Sheol surrounded me; the snares of death confronted me. In my distress I called upon the Lord, and cried out to my God; He heard my voice from His temple, and my cry came before Him, even to His ears (Psalm 18:4–6).

An Extra Helping

If you have a prison minister, ask if he can get permission from the jail for each prisoner to have a treat. Upwards of a thousand are easy to do with one congregation of willing workers if they assemble it the following way:

- 1 brown bag
- 1 standard-sized candy bar
- 1 travel-size toothpaste
- 1 Bible chart from BibleCharts.org

You will be surprised how much joy can be spread this way, and how thankful their hearts are.

> I am weary with my groaning; all night I make my bed swim; I drench my couch with my tears. My eye wastes away because of grief; it grows old because of all my enemies.
>
> Depart from me, all you workers of iniquity; for the Lord has heard the voice of my weeping. The Lord has heard my supplication; the Lord will receive my prayer (Psalm 6:6–9).

These suffice to show the power of pouring out your heart to God in song (Psalm 62:8), but one psalm contrasts despair with triumph like no other. That's because it's a prophetic glance into the ultimate darkest moment in all of time followed by the exuberant realization of the eternal joy that was born from that moment.

> My strength is dried up like a potsherd, and My tongue clings to My jaws; you have brought Me to the dust of death. For dogs have surrounded Me; the congregation of the wicked has enclosed Me. They pierced My hands and My feet; I can count all My bones. They look and stare at Me. They divide My garments among them, and for My clothing they cast lots . . . I will declare Your name to My brethren; in the midst of the assembly I will praise You. You who fear the Lord, praise Him! All you descendants of Jacob, glorify Him, and fear Him, all you offspring of Israel! For He has not despised nor abhorred the affliction of the afflicted; nor has He hidden His face from Him; but when He cried to Him, He heard. My praise shall be of You in the great assembly (Psalm 22:15–18, 22–25).

Prisoners Were Listening

I once heard of a Christian lady who had been kidnapped and locked in a trunk. When recounting her survival, she said that she sang familiar hymns the whole time. I've known of many Christians on their deathbed who brought forth song when they could barely speak. In Angola, Louisiana State Penitentiary inmates who have been changed by the gospel of Christ gather to strengthen one another by singing *Jesus Loves Me*. It was good enough for Paul and Silas; it's good enough for Angola; it's good enough for me.

But my favorite part of the whole story just may be, "And the prisoners were listening to them" (Acts 16:25). Without Christ, people are imprisoned by their own sin. Jesus said, "Most assuredly, I say to you, whoever commits sin is a slave of sin" (John 8:34). Prison conditions are clear in passages like Proverbs 23:31–35 and 2 Peter 2:12–14. Sin slaves are trapped in hopeless circumstances and await eternal doom.

What are those down the prison halls from you hearing? Are you living a life in front of them that sings out the escape they are looking for? Are the prisoners listening to you? Paul and Silas were unable to go from cell to cell for an open Bible study, but their out-loud joy which surpassed the surroundings preached a sermon to these prisoners.

Having a bad hair day that somehow spread to the rest of your body and out into the atmosphere? It might not be as bad as you think. Paul and Silas's bad night led to a houseful of baptisms. Sing loud and pray hard. You haven't even had your earthquake yet.

Indeed we count them blessed who endure.
—James 5:11

1. Research ancient prisons. Which aspect strikes you as particularly hard or cruel? How does it give you new insight to this story?

2. If possible at all—I didn't say if comfortable—sit on the floor resting your feet six to twelve inches off the floor on some object.

Keep your feet straight up. How long can you last in this position? I'll even let you watch the news or another TV program—something Paul and Silas couldn't do—to ease the strain. Go as long as you can, and then discuss with others in your group study or elsewhere how it felt. Do you think the Roman prison conditions weakened Paul and Silas, strengthened them, or both?

3. What are some other rote pieces of prayer that we use often? Pick one, and revisit what that phrase actually means. How can we rephrase it to fit our specific circumstances a little better, and get us more on a one-on-one circuit with our God and Father?

4. Which familiar song do you turn to for comfort when emotional pain blocks all other resources? Examine the words of the song again, and what it is about them that mean so much to you. Swap these sentiments in your group study or among close friends.

5. Take a look at the Psalms again. What other psalms not mentioned begin with disparaging words but follow through with a reversal and end in words of confident hope?

6. Notice Psalm 22:25 says, "My praise shall be of You in the great assembly." Where is our praise sometimes misdirected in assembly? How do our results differ from those of the psalmist because of it? Are these internal results, external results, or both?

7. Consider Hebrews 2:11–12, which references the above Psalm. What conclusion do we come to about who is harmonizing with us in our singing? How should that impact the passion of our song service?

A Favorite Piece

And speaking of a broken-down van . . .

Everybody knows you don't look in the Yellow Pages, not for a really good mechanic. You have to hear about him through a chain of cousins, neighbors, and the deacon over bus ministry. It's ironic that the vehicle that hours ago you didn't trust to take you to the corner Walmart, you now drive thirty miles down a country road and two more miles down a dirt one, hoping and praying that the universal joint doesn't just completely drop out on the twenty-ninth mile. Each cow stares more than the one before.

Dad trained me well on finding the most remote possible repairman, which is hard to do when you live in a metropolis the size of Birmingham. How many off-roads could there be? We found them. Up an alley between Forty-First and Forty-Second Street—Who knew the streets were numbered that high?—there was the remnant of a house behind which was a dinged-up garage with "upholestree" spray-painted on the side. The guy could patch up a back seat damaged by four kids and a collie for a song. I think the song was *Purple Haze* by Jimi Hendrix, but he got the job done.

Yeah—the best ones are off the beaten path, and we have found a host of them through the years, but you have to wait in line to use them. They don't seem to need a computer sensor to determine your problem. They pull a socket wrench out of a rusty refrigerator converted to an upright tool chest and get down to business.

Our current mechanic shop is down Homer Lee Douglas Road, and forget about even trying to use your cell phone there. It doesn't matter what time we arrive; we're greeted by a three-legged dog named Valvoline, and eight puppies. We

153

know just to leave the keys under the mat with a note about the problem.

My husband's notes are reasonable—he has a little background in an auto parts store. Me? I thought shocks and struts had something to do with the Miss America pageant. My notes sound something like this:

> I was driving to the field trip, and my daughter noticed something that sounded like when we dropped the metal collection plate in church. I'm not sure if it's related, but there's a little doo-dah hanging down under the car close to that grey long thing, but maybe it's supposed to. I put some scotch tape on it, but I don't think it held. I only have sixty-two dollars, so call me if it's more than that.

It doesn't matter when we pick the car up either. If they're there, they're open. If they're not there, leave the check in the right desk drawer. I'm serious.

We have never had a problem leaving our keys under the mat or leaving checks lying around. However, once during midlife crisis, my dad had the crazy urge to do something wild he had missed out on in youth, like take a car to a recognized national chain. It was just a one-night thing, just once, but I kid you not, the car was stolen.

I guess all the thrill rides to back alleys for upholstery jobs and brake pads had an impact on my brother because he went the route of mechanics. He's a whiz at diagnosis, but he's disaster for the living room carpet and couch.

I recently took my car in twice for power steering trouble, still with no results. It wasn't necessarily giving me any problems; it just sounded like Jar Jar Binks on helium.

We were beating various car parts under the hood with a hairbrush. Who carries a wrench in her purse?

154

I turned a lot of heads as I arrived in grand fashion at Thanksgiving dinner. My brother said, "You need to invest 2.98 in a bottle of Power Flush; where's the sweet potatoes?" It fixed it completely, 322 dollars too late.

But there's something in addition to expertise. Some of these people just have the magic touch. My sister and I were hindered from a grocery store run when we were teens because the car wouldn't start. My brother popped the hood, gave the battery terminal a couple of taps with a wrench, and voila! He made it look so easy. We were not as successful in the grocery store parking lot after we had purchased the ice cream in 97-degree weather—and that was Celsius I think—when we were beating various car parts under the hood with a hairbrush. Who carries a wrench in her purse?

So next time your car leaves you stranded, look for a garage with a big ad spray-painted on the side, instead of in the yellow pages. But don't stay too long or you might come home with a puppy named Duralast.

CHAPTER 12

Makes Me
Love Everybody

(And That's the Greatest Part of All)

"**H**ow much do you love me?" It's a burning question that we all have to know, but has anyone ever given a satisfactory answer? A song from *Guys and Dolls* answers, "A bushel and a peck." How would you really feel about that? How about if your husband loves you one bushel and one peck? That's like being worth 124 corn cobs plus whatever a peck is.

Sometimes someone will stretch his arms out and say, "I love you this much." Well, of course it's that much. Whoever separated his arms the size of a twelve-inch ruler and said, "Honey, I love you this much"? By saying, "I love you this much," he is committing himself to opening his arms all the way. But then how much is his arm span? If your friend's husband's arm span is 58 inches, and your husband's is 54 inches, does her husband love her more than yours loves you?

And so we do the comparison thing. "I love you more than chocolate cheesecake." *Wow,* you think, *that's really a lot. That's a lot more than brownies, even, but not as much as cherry dump cake.* It's kind of a downer to be loved less than something with dump in its title.

> But God demonstrates His own love toward us, in that while we were still sinners, Christ died for us (Romans 5:8).

A Higher Definition

And so we struggle with the "how much do you love me" question, but God has no problem answering it. "Greater love has no one than this, than to lay down one's life for his friends" (John 15:13). How much? Can I have a demonstration of that?

". . . while we were still sinners, Christ died for us" (Romans 5:8).

There is no greater love than giving your life for a friend, and yet Christ did more than that—He gave it for those who were not His friends. He gave it for us, while we were just plain sinners, not friends. He loved more than the greatest love. God can do that.

Does that old time religion, as the song says, make me love everybody? It should. Love is the theme of the Bible, the heart of the gospel, the essence of God (1 John 4:8).

Ever heard someone say, "All my preacher wants to preach on is love"? If he's preaching something else, he's not a gospel preacher. You can't talk about the plan of salvation without talking about love. You can't preach about Jesus without preaching love. It's impossible to worship without love. You can't think about hell or heaven without being keenly aware of love rescuing you from one and landing you in the other. And there's no such thing as evangelism without love. Love permeates everything in the Christian walk.

The only thing left for your preacher to preach about is Batman or grape jelly.

Tokens of Love

There's a big difference in a congregation where love is spoken out loud, and one where it is rarely brought up, if at all. I have a construction paper heart on my refrigerator that has been there twenty-three years. It has changed refrigerators once, and houses six times. We first got it when an elder stood before the congregation we were leaving because they were sending us to a stateside mission point that had a church of nine people. "Put this heart on your refrigerator," he said, "and every time you see it, remember how many people there are at home who love you." I'm sure he has no idea that it's still there, but we took him at his word. We still look at it twenty-three years later, and we still think about how many people love us. We have a quilt and a bowl and maybe some other things that were going-away gifts at various places. All of them are great, but none surpass the value of that faded paper heart.

My husband has a similar three-word note, "Preach, Brother, Preach!" that the song leader slipped him years ago just before he got up to speak. It's in his Bible to this day. Christians thrive in a congregation where brothers hug and sisters hug, and you can't get out the door without someone reminding you again, "I love you." God is all over that place. Listen to 1 John 4:7–8.

> Beloved, let us love one another, for love is of God; and everyone who loves is born of God and knows God. He who does not love does not know God, for God is love.

Did you pick up on that last sentence? What happens in those congregations that don't give away paper hearts and encouraging notes, hugs, and love reminders?

"Put this heart on your refrigerator and every time you see it, remember how many people love you."

159

What's going on in those walls? From what I've seen, this: suspicion, mistrust, division, fights over which vacuum cleaner to keep and which one to throw away, whispering, eye-rolling, and finally, going separate ways and putting a new name above the door. It's hard to find God there even on a Lord's Day. He doesn't come because He's not invited. If you get anything out of 1 John 4:7–8, get those last three words: God is love. Where love is not present, neither is God.

> Which is the first commandment
> of all? (Mark 12:28).

Lord, Tell Me One Thing

Won't it be great to meet Jesus in person? I have never yet even visited what are referred to as the Holy Lands in the Middle East, but we often talk about how grand it would be just to walk the same ground that Jesus himself once walked, to envision Him sitting on that rock over there or stepping into a boat on this very bank. That's how we long for glimpses into His life, but we have a reel full of glimpses sitting on our nightstand.

What would you ask Him? If you had just one opportunity to be there near the fig trees and the river banks about AD 31, and you were able to break through the crowds or climb up in the tree, wouldn't you love to say, "Lord, tell me the one thing, the most important thing, out of all your teaching, and all of scripture. What is it, Jesus?"

It would be nice to do that, but it's already been done, and we have the answer in that glimpse-reel I mentioned on our nightstand. Open up to Mark 12:28 where a scribe asks Jesus the same question. The answer is to love God fully, completely (vv. 29–30). But Jesus gives a bonus answer, while He's on the greatest subject of all. "And the second, like it, is this: 'You shall love your neighbor as yourself.' There is no other commandment greater than these" (v. 31).

Loving God and loving everyone else are so intertwined that Jesus couldn't even discuss one without the other. In the same chapter where John tells us God is love, just a little later he says,

> If someone says, "I love God," and hates his brother, he is a liar; for he who does not love his brother whom he has seen, how can he love God whom he has not seen? (1 John 4:20).

The Heart of the Letter

What is the love chapter of the Bible? Every chapter. But our automatic response to that question is 1 Corinthians 13. Look at its location. It was written to Corinthian Christians, the congregation with all the problems. If there had been a magazine called *Spiritual Immaturity Quarterly*, their picture would have been on the cover. Paul spends chapter 12 combating the apparently prevalent attitude there that "some of us are just a little bit better than most of y'all." Chapter 12 ends with Paul's saying, "And yet I show you a more excellent way." And remember, there were no chapter divisions in the original letter.

Following chapter 13, Paul addresses the circus nature of the assemblies because so many of the Corinthians were calling attention to themselves, and they were still measuring "my gifts against your gifts." Isn't it incredibly interesting that the "love chapter" of the Bible is wedged in here? Look at the rest of the book. Paul calls them carnal and spiritual infants, they're defiling their own bodies (ch. 3), and they're bragging about parading adultery around in front of the world (ch. 5). It wasn't a "feel good" inspirational letter.

Should we talk about love all the time? The Holy Spirit couldn't even correct a congregation concerning adultery, marriage questions (ch. 7), stinginess in supporting preachers (ch. 9), flagrant misuse of the Lord's supper (ch. 11), and questions about the resurrection (ch. 15) without writing a thorough treatise on love.

It's the heart of the letter. I'm sure the Corinthians claimed a loving spirit, but such problems don't stem from a loving spirit, so Paul in essence says, "I think you may be a little confused about

Love Where You Live

Love cleans up the fourth spill at the supper table without lashing out. Love listens to the entire plot of a Pokémon episode without yawning. *Love suffers long.*

Love kisses boo-boos, rocks crying babies, and sews eyes back on teddy bears. *Love is kind.*

When love looks at the Gucci bag and the perfect lipstick and the 14-karat earrings of her sister on the pew, and then looks down at her milk-stained diaper bag where she can't tell lipstick from a broken crayon, and feels her ears to find one lone earring after that upside-down communion thing, *love envies not.*

Love stays up three nights in a row making costumes for the kindergarten play, and her name does not appear on the program. *Love vaunts not itself.*

Love cheers the loudest at the tee-ball game, puts a torn-out notebook page of a lopsided heart on the center of the fridge, and claps the longest at the curtain call, and at the end of the day gives God the glory in a faded tee-shirt of a nightgown and a quiet, thankful voice. *Love is not puffed up.*

Love does not argue with the referees in front of the whole junior high. *Love does not behave itself unseemly.*

Love misses the half-price sale for the piano recital. *Love seeks not her own.*

what love is." The world is confused about what love is, and lest we get caught up in the confusion, let's take a look at 1 Corinthians 13. It's really not a flowery, sugary, touchy-feely, floating-on-air abstract concept that you can't help. It's kindness, patience, and endurance on purpose. And you can walk in a congregation and

Love dashes up the stairs to frantic shrieks of panic only to find there is a ladybug on the mirror. *Love is not easily provoked.*

Love tries to forget the time that her Snow Village was demolished with a Tonka Crane, the time a red sock was dried with her new white shirt, and the time her azalea was watered with the gas can. *Love takes no account of evil.*

Love spends Saturday nights cutting out Noah's arks and memorizing beatitudes. Love drives four hours in the middle of the night to a summer Bible camp swimming pool to watch something that lasts five seconds. It is the greatest event of her life. *Love rejoices in the truth.*

Love changes sheets in the middle of the night and camps out in the rain with the cub scouts. *Love bears all things.*

Love knows that one day he will remember to put the lid back down. One day he will tighten the top of the 2-liter. One day he will know his shoes are untied without anyone telling him. *Love believes all things.*

Love prays for a little girl she doesn't even know who will one day steal her son away from her. Love's heart beats off the scale when her son is on the free-throw line. *Love hopes all things.*

Love eats potted meat all week to buy a used saxophone for seventh grade band. *Love endures all things.*

Love is there when the boyfriend is crummy, the spelling bee is lost, the package didn't come, and there are monsters under the bed . . . *Love never fails.*

know if it's there by knowing what it's not, according to this chapter. It's not rude; it doesn't insist on its own way; it doesn't boast.

> Love never fails (1 Corinthians 13:8).

Love on the Rocks

How do we get that down to Wednesday night and Thursday morning in the twenty-first century? It crosses cultural lines easily. None of these concepts are foreign ones that worked only within a twenty-mile radius of Aphrodite's temple in Corinth. They transfer well into our ladies' day meetings where your idea is better than mine, into Bible camp the last half of the week when there may be a temptation to become irritable, to sitting up in ICU waiting rooms that are cold and chairs that are hard because love bears all things. More than anything, these traits should transfer beautifully into our Christian homes.

In Peter's closing thoughts of his letter to first century Christians, he said, "And above all things have fervent love for one another, for 'love will cover a multitude of sins'" (1 Peter 4:8). Peter's letter had addressed a number of important topics, but there's one "above all" idea, and it's love.

A Truth That Sustains

Does old time religion make me love everybody? If it's old enough. But there are some people who are harder to love than others. Some seem to get a thrill out of trying my patience, being abrasive, turning a joyous occasion into a contentious one. How can we do it?

> But God demonstrates His own love toward us, in that while we were still sinners, Christ died for us (Romans 5:8).

How Can We Not Do It?

In 1940 my dad and his ten brothers and sisters, his mama and papa, and their mule were uprooted from their home in Peaceburg, Alabama. Fort McClellan acquired the land for battle practice, and the government forced residents to leave. I've always thought it was interesting that a town with peace as its name would be closed down for the purposes of war.

Sometimes the government will open the land for a day so that a dwindling number of former residents—those who were children then are aged now—can go and remember. My dad will point out a tree, and envision where his home once sat in relation to the tree, but everything is gone. Almost.

There is one set of concrete steps which, for some reason, survived all the bombs, the grenades, the warfare. It is the only piece of any structure that remains. The steps once led to the door of the Peaceburg Church of Christ building, and as you draw near to take a closer look, there is something unmistakably etched on the steps. It simply says, "God is love."

An Extra Helping

Love *does*, so make your vehicle a mop-mobile. In demonstrating our love, we often ask the question, "What can I do?" It's a good one because we never know if dishes need washing or meds need refilling or dry cleaning needs to be picked up. But one truth is constant: the floor needs mopping! Keep a mop, a bucket, and a bottle of detergent in the trunk of your car. (Add a towel if you need to dry the floor for fall-risk friends.)

It doesn't take long to mop a kitchen, so when you ring a doorbell, have your supplies already in hand, and say something like, "I had fifteen minutes between errands today, so my favorite way to spend them is with you."

It stands the hair up on your arm with the keen realization that life can rob you of house and home. Bombs may drop and destroy the foundation of your life as you're accustomed to it, but one earth-shattering truth remains that can sustain you through life everlasting (Romans 8:38–39).

God is love.

> *For I am persuaded that neither death nor life, nor angels nor principalities nor powers, nor things present nor things to come, nor height nor depth, nor any other created thing, shall be able to separate us from the love of God which is in Christ Jesus our Lord.*
> —Romans 8:38–39

Soul Food

1. In perfecting your love to match its definition in 1 Corinthians 13, which characteristic needs the most work for you personally? Pray about it every day this week, but in addition, look at your calendar and see when and where you think this will be challenged the most. In being aware of the challenge, determine to exemplify that one characteristic, "above all."

2. How many times does the Bible say to love your neighbor as yourself?

3. List four of the above passages that say in so many words that all commands are basically summed up in the two love commands. How so? Make a list of specific commands in the Old or New Testament which would not have to be stated if we really loved God, and our neighbor as ourselves.

4. There have been several inspirational articles, books, and speeches which have related the above passages to self-esteem. If these passages are related to self-esteem, show how they are.

5. Meeting Jesus in person and asking Him a question is mentioned. The "greatest command" question is not the only one brought to Him in the Gospels. Make a list of other questions asked of Him. Of these, which one would you have been likely to ask had you been in one of those crowds? Take His answer and treasure it as His own conversation with you. Write it down and carry it in your purse. Memorize it, dwell on it daily, and commit to live it.

6. Of faith, hope, and love, why is love the greatest?

7. What problems, in addition to those listed, did the church in Corinth have? Is it fair to say that Corinth claimed the gold on church problems, or do you think there are other New Testament congregations which paralleled it? If so, which ones, and why?

8. A "home edition" of 1 Corinthians 13 is given. Rewrite it to match the events going on in your home, which demand the attributes of 1 Corinthians 13 love.

9. At the end of 1 Corinthians 12 Paul says, "And yet I show you a more excellent way." Compare spiritual gifts, which were amazing, to love, which should be commonplace. List the ways in which love is more excellent than these powerful gifts.

10. Is there a passage in the Old or New Testament that you struggle with because, at first read, it seems that God is unloving? Take that event and reverse in your mind God's action at that point. What would

In perfecting your love to match its Corinthians definition, which characteristic needs the most work for you?

have unfolded in the future had God's decision or action been different? Is it possible that the seemingly harsh thing was an extremely difficult, loving thing to do?

A Favorite Piece

And speaking of construction paper hearts . . .

It happens. Seven years ago, my son fussed at his friends all the way to the creek on the revered "Hike Night" at summer Bible camp. It was the only time all week you were allowed to hold hands with a girl, but that didn't mean for one minute that he was going to do it. He let his friends know what he thought of their betrayal to the code in no uncertain terms, and you could hear his badgering voice clear to the bank.

"I can't believe you're doing this. You'll never see me walking down the road holding hands with a girl." He was relentless.

But it happens. I couldn't help but reflect on that as I glanced across the gym this past summer at his table. It was "Banquet Night" at the university's summer youth camp, and he was all dressed up at a table that was conspicuously boy, girl, boy, girl, boy, girl. He wasn't giving speeches to the other guys this time.

You've got to love God's plan for romance from the beginning. What happened the first time Adam saw Eve? There were flowers in abundance that had waited three long days to be picked. I wonder what that first awkward bouquet looked like. One thing was sure. While Eve was smiling on the outside, she wasn't thinking, "These smell like a funeral" or "I'd rather have chocolate!"

Something settles through the years, and you wonder if by the time Seth was born, Adam brought home a gift-wrapped—or not—set of new shoes for the camel with a five-year warranty when their anniversary rolled around. It happens.

I'd rather stand in line for a day and a half between a talk show host and a chicken truck than to relive the dating years, but looking back, there's a pitiful, sweet amusement to the scene. I had more than my share of Valentine's Days where I longed for a stuffed gorilla with huge red lips like the other girls in my class had, or a balloon tied to my locker, but what I got was heart-shaped teacakes from my mom. Wow, I can't even write that without the keen realization of how messed-up my priorities were. Now it's bring on the teacakes; donate the gorillas!

On carnation day, guys could buy flowers from the Beta Club and have them delivered to a girl right in the middle of class. Some girls could make a homecoming float with their winnings. I didn't have any trouble carrying my books to the bus—no flowers in the way there.

And then at 4:30 there was a knock at my door from the kid who had bought me a flower but had been too scared to give it to me. As he stood there in his thick glasses and flood pants, all I could say was, "Thank you." He thought it was for the flower. It was really for not doing this in front of everyone at school.

We grew up, and he's a great guy. It happens.

As the years passed so did the fleeting romances. The names are there, but the details escape me. Except for Peter. Peter picked me up in his mother's ginormous Wagoneer an hour and a half late because he had run out of gas on the way. I knew if my parents saw his mother's bumper sticker—ERA Yes!— they wouldn't let me go with him, so I jumped in and we hurried away to the nearest restaurant: Pizza Hut.

It had to always be the nearest restaurant with Peter because his parents charged him twenty cents per mile to use their vehicle. He parked it as soon as he turned off the highway, hardly even in the parking lot, much less in a space, and if we decided to go anywhere else beside the restaurant on the date, we always walked to avoid adding twenty more cents to the tab.

That first catastrophic date Peter stuck the straw up his nose instead of in his mouth and also strangled on his drink, water, which was twenty cents cheaper than gas. I worried he might ask for a to-go box for the crusts, and save that for our next date. But I found something about him very sweet and fun. It happens.

That was long before the final romance—the one that stuck. It was every bit as awkward as every one before, trying to casually take a sip from the Arby's sauce, thinking it was my drink. I was won by homemade cards that would have sent Martha Stewart to the cardiac unit, long wades in the creek, and well-done macaroni and cheese from a box. I think there is far more to be cherished in the effort to be romantic than in the end product.

It's why I love Valentine's Day. I know and meet people who don't care so much for it, and I understand . . . too much commercialism, maybe some have bad memories. But I wonder if they've ever been given a lopsided construction-paper heart mounted with glue-stick to a torn out piece of notebook paper, if they've ever served spaghetti in a church basement to white-haired couples dressed in bright red sweaters, holding wrinkled hands, and knowing more about romance than Harlequin ever did.

Have they ever pretended just for a moment to like chalk-flavored hearts that say "U R Cute"? There's just something extra sweet about Valentine's Day. It's a celebration of love, romance, and marriage in a world where those things aren't valued nearly as much as they should be.

Yes, we ought to celebrate love and marriage the other 364 days of the year,

I worried he might ask for a to-go box for the crusts, and save that for our next date.

too, but I just can't knock the one day we do set aside to honor it. So give it a whirl, whether it's for that lifelong companion who leaves his drawers on the floor and his life in your heart; or that little guy who loves pirates, transformers, and you; or that person down the street that you just met—go ahead. Burn some brownies, spill glue on a lopsided heart, plan a romantic evening, and get a nosebleed trying to sip from a straw as you look in his eyes.

It happens.

It Will Do Me When
I'm Dying
(But Will I Do It
When I'm Living?)

Because Two Things Are Certain,
and Taxes Is Not One of Them

Where were you last time you thought about it? I was sitting on the exit row of a Boeing 737 when they asked me if I understood what to do to assist other passengers in the event of an emergency. I nodded, but inside I thought, *We are all going to die.*

The deal is, we *are* all going to die. I hate to end the book on this chapter, but then again, I hate not to. We don't think about it enough. We don't talk about it enough. "It is appointed to men once to die, but after this, the judgment" (Hebrews 9:27 KJV). I'm on my way to that appointment, and the only thing that is going to stop me from getting there is for the Lord to come first. Either way, the judgment part is still there.

If we thought about death and its certain but untimely arrival more often, how would we play out the days differently?

This people honors Me with their lips, but their heart is far from Me (Mark 7:6).

Two Kinds: Artificial or the Real Thing

The old song is talking about religion when it says, "It will do me when I'm dying." Will it? Religion has such a bad taste in people's mouth, but it's because most of them don't know there are two kinds of religion—true religion and false religion.

Artificial sweetener tastes bad. I'm sorry, you may like it, but it tastes bad. If you like it, it's because you have acquired a taste for it. But true sweetener tastes good from the first time you dip the pacifier in it.

Artificial religion is found in Matthew 15:9 and Mark 7:7 with those who are "teaching as doctrines the commandments of men." There are thirty-nine verses of artificial religion in Matthew 23, and Jesus doesn't think it tastes good at all. He calls those who swim in it blind and fools. Artificial religion tastes so bad in Revelation 3:16 that it causes the Lord to vomit.

So I understand. It's no wonder that so many say that they love God but don't want any part of religion. It's because they've never had the real thing. James 1:27 gives us a pretty good description of true religion,

Pure and undefiled religion before God and the Father is this: to visit orphans and widows in their trouble, and to keep oneself unspotted from the world.

Now what's distasteful about that? We have a beautiful description of helping children and older people, and of staying pure. Sounds like you could sum it up in the phrase "living right."

Do It When You're Living

If I want a religion that will do me when I'm dying, I've got to make sure I do it when I'm living. Look at James 1:27 again. The last part gets lost in our lives sometimes, but then so does the first part.

I don't want to find myself dying and think that I never really did step in and help people who were living, and living in trouble. Have you adopted an orphan? I thank God for your on-purpose love that changes a life and an eternity. Are you a foster parent? There are no heroes in my book that stand taller than you. But even if your circumstances aren't so you can do that, or you're afraid to bite off quite that much, you can do James 1:27—the A part.

Not terribly long ago, an elder in the church mentioned that he felt challenged to follow the command in this verse because he didn't know any true orphans. The word means fatherless and is translated that way in a number of versions. You may have to look around awhile to find an orphan like the ones in the movies, who have lost both parents to a fire or some other tragedy—though there are some of those around as well—but you won't have to draw a very big circle around where your feet are to find someone who's fatherless in it. He is a child without a provider, a child who doesn't know who his father is, a child whose father is in prison, a child whose father is seen more high or drunk than sober. If you don't see that in our society, then maybe your religion is like that in Matthew 23, because I don't see how you could be anything but blind.

They are scattered throughout our pews, and we may not make a legal

You won't have to draw a very big circle around where your feet are to find someone who's fatherless.

arrangement for their care, but in the congregation, homes are open for them to come in and out of, tables are spread whenever they're around, they have full backpacks in the fall, toys at Christmas, new clothes at Easter, a Bible with their name on it, and years worth of hugs and tears, phone calls and church rides, and worn-out cards and candy wrappers to look back on and fill their hearts for life.

Now what is it people hate about religion?

> Do you not know that friendship with the world is enmity with God? (James 4:4).

Wearing Stylish Spots?

The B-part is just as valuable. It's what a Father wants for His child. There has never been anything good for us about impurities. How much salmonella do you want in your salad? Wouldn't you like just a cup of cold water from the part of the creek that has stagnated and smells of dead fish?

We treat our dog better than that. We want to make sure her water is changed every day, and when she comes home smelling like the finest in road kill, there's only one thing to be done—hold our noses and get a bucket of suds.

What about when it comes to our children? Just how many spots would we like for them to have? Alcoholism? Not the whole blotch, just a little drink. Fornication? Not the diseases or anything, just a little lust. Profanity? Not the big ones, just the little ones. Our kids in the church smell like road kill to their Father because we've got just a little bit of algae and dead fish in the water. We need a big bucket of suds, and a lot of determination to stay out of there and to keep "unspotted from the world."

But it's not just our children. Somehow, peer pressure doesn't go away somewhere in your early twenties. Somehow, the drive to be exactly like everyone around you, if anything, intensifies. It is us, the grown-ups, who are caught up in whose hair bow is the prettiest—which seems innocent enough—until it translates into whose convertible is the shiniest, and even though we told ourselves when they were little that this would never happen, we find ourselves investing hundreds of dollars at one pop on the evening gown that will draw the most attention to a body. We sing "Seek Ye First" loud and clear at our assemblies, as long as we realize that everyone understands we really mean second.

Live Like You're Dying

The tug is for us to immerse our children in the world, but the greater pull is for us to also follow suit. Alcohol has become a fashionable spot, and many of us who were able to avoid it in high school and college have now been defeated by the pressure. It's just hard to meet after work for drinks time after time and be the only one who's not having one. We can no longer lean on "my mother will kill me," so instead of battling our conscience, we have decided to change our convictions. Proverbs 23:31 hasn't changed, Proverbs 20:1 hasn't changed, 1 Peter 4:3 hasn't changed, God hasn't changed (Hebrews 13:8), but we'd like just a little salmonella in our salad now.

Idolatry has also become a stylish spot. "No other gods before me" is now rendered "only select gods before me." These gods are the ones who offer great promise in this life, that only come around once, or that we've already invested a bunch of money in before we realized they would interfere. We have become so involved in living, that we're forgetting that we're dying.

Be Scared

Preachers used to remind people at the end of every sermon that they might just die tonight, and then what? In those days, the front row could fill up by the first chorus of the song because people wanted to make sure they were living right so they could make sure they were dying right.

But that's when hell was as real as heaven. Again, there's part of me that wants to start and finish this book without ever visiting this terrible thought, but that's the part of me that Satan's got a hold on. It's just not acceptable to let two children race on horseback down a pretty road without telling them that a very tall bridge is out around the bend.

I don't want to use scare tactics, but I don't have to. God already has. Scripture says:

> And do not fear those who kill the body but cannot kill the soul. But rather fear Him who is able to destroy both soul and body in hell (Matthew 10:28).

> Then He will also say to those on the left hand, "Depart from Me, you cursed, into the everlasting fire prepared for the devil and his angels" (Matthew 25:41).

> And being in torments in Hades, he lifted up his eyes and saw Abraham afar off, and Lazarus in his bosom. Then he cried and said, "Father Abraham, have mercy on me, and send Lazarus that he may dip the tip of his finger in water and cool my tongue; for I am tormented in this flame." But Abraham said, "Son, remember

An Extra Helping

Help your child (or a child within your influence) make a construction paper chain with one word on each strip making the sentence "We ought to obey God rather than men" from Acts 5:29. Hang this on the bedpost and add links to it through the years every time your child uses this principle to triumph over temptation. Let the child date each link and record a precious memory, i.e. "Left the ball field during the last inning. Loved Bible class (Baalam)"; "Stayed home because the movie they were watching was R. Made cookies. Watched Kung Fu Panda."

that in your lifetime you received your good things, and likewise Lazarus evil things; but now he is comforted and you are tormented" (Luke 16:23–25).

In flaming fire taking vengeance on those who do not know God, and on those who do not obey the gospel of our Lord Jesus Christ. These shall be punished with everlasting destruction from the presence of the Lord and from the glory of His power (2 Thessalonians 1:8–9).

A keen awareness of hell and heaven doesn't make life a downer; it makes death an upper. Suddenly, because we constantly remind ourselves that there is an eternal destination beyond thirty-year annuities and the World Series, we're caught up in the right things. We're ready.

For we know that if our earthly house, this tent, is destroyed, we have a building from God, a house not made with hands, eternal in the heavens (2 Corinthians 5:1).

Bring it on! "O death, where is thy sting? O grave, where is thy victory?" (1 Corinthians 15:55 KJV).

No matter how I try to phrase it, I can't come up with anything better or more succinct than "to live is Christ, and to die is gain" (Philippians 1:21).

What Really Matters?

"To die will be an awfully big adventure." It was said by Peter Pan (Barrie 87), but it rings truer than fairy tale. "Set your affection on things above, not on things on the earth" (Colossians 3:2 KJV).

My sister Sami says, "Always remember three little words: *It doesn't matter.*" And she's right. Whatever doesn't make a difference in eternity doesn't make a difference at all. It doesn't matter if you get the dress smocked in time for Easter; it doesn't matter if company comes when it looks like something large in your den with many parts must have exploded; it doesn't matter if you wreck the new Mercedes! It doesn't matter, but how you view these things does. How it surfaced that in the midst of all these things you were distracted by pure religion and undefiled before God and the Father—that is going to matter for generations on earth and eternity on the other side.

Don't let the liar, and the father of it (John 8:44) play his trump card. It's this one (though he phrases it a little prettier): No matter how selfishly a person lives her life, though she may laugh at religion and carelessly wreck a number of lives along the way and never repent, because we somehow hate to think about eternal torment for anyone, and because we care for that person on some level, everything's going to be okay, and God's mercy will take that person to heaven where she will be smiling down on us.

It's a nice thought, but it's blasphemy—direct opposition to the loving truth of God, who seeks to warn and save us from that thinking to the degree that He would send His own Son to die for us, if we will only repent and obey. The answer to hell is not to ignore it and it will go away. The answer is the calming, soothing one of John 14.

> Let not your heart be troubled; you believe in God, believe also in Me. In My Father's house are many mansions; if it were not so, I would have told you. I go to prepare a place for you. And if I go and prepare a place for you, I will come again and receive you to Myself; that where I am, there you may be also (John 14:1–3).

Don't let the liar, and the father of it play his trump card.

At this point Thomas said that He didn't know the way to this place, and we all know Jesus' answer. "I am the way, the truth, and the life. No one comes to the Father except through Me." You can't get there just any old way. At least four times, Jesus communicates one thought throughout the rest of that chapter. It's this: *If you love me, keep my commandments.* Four times? Really? When's the last time you told a friend something four times before she walked out the door? Oh, it was the time that whatever it was, it was absolutely crucial for her to remember.

> Why are you troubled? And why do doubts arise in your hearts? Luke 24:38).

No Troubled Hearts

If you want to get to that prepared place, it's crucial to remember to keep those commandments. "Now by this we know that we know Him, if we keep His commandments" (1 John 2:3). We don't have to wonder if we're going to "make it." We know. In the same chapter that Jesus said four times to keep His commandments, He began and ended the discussion with, "Let not your heart be troubled" (John 14:1, 27), and somewhere in the middle, He said, "I will not leave you orphans; I will come to you" (v. 18). How interesting that in busying ourselves with caring for the fatherless physically, we are assuring that we never become such spiritually.

Several years ago, a family in the mission field was threatened with a huge tsunami. It was nearly certain that there would be few survivors, and there was little time or means to escape. When asked what they were doing in such dire straits, their answer was, "Eating toast and jelly." Their hearts were not troubled, their hope was sure, and their one thought was bigger than a tsunami . . .

"To die will be an awfully big adventure."

For our citizenship is in heaven, from which we also eagerly wait
for the Savior, the Lord Jesus Christ, who will transform our
lowly body that it may be conformed to His glorious body.
—Philippians 3:20–21

Soul Food

1. Make a list of at least five ancient Greek or Roman gods. In a column next to these, put what each of these gods promised (rain, love, wealth, etc.). Is there anything in that column which Jehovah God has not already provided? Now make a list of current-day cultural gods, and in the column next to each put what this idol promises. What on that list is worth forfeiting everlasting life for, and which is worth accepting eternal condemnation in exchange?

2. It's easy for life to distract us from the spiritual, but how much better is it to be distracted from the everyday hysteria by a spiritual focus. In the past week, what specific "small stuff" have you sweated when you should have let it go ruling in favor of the bigger, better picture? How will this realization help you react differently next time?

3. Proverbs 23:29 asks six questions. Do any of the six represent what any of us want? Read through verse 35 and determine what it is that keeps people seeking what no one wants.

4. Have you ever returned food or drink in a restaurant, refusing to eat it because of impurities. Share the story if you are in a group study. How does this relate to pure and undefiled religion?

5. How do you feel about the phrase, *It Doesn't Matter*? If we swallow this whole, we could be persuaded to be a slacker on the job or to never encourage our children to study in school. But why, in light of eternity, would job performance or academic excellence be an *It Does Matter*? On the flip side, if a Christian loses a job or fails a test, how does a spiritual focus help her get through that?

A Favorite Piece

And speaking of a trump card . . .

Who knew? How did it come about? Who invented this? I mean, when Eliphaz, Bildad and Zophar came to see Job, did each bring a deck of cards to pass the seven days of silence? Somewhere at some point back in time, someone with a very arbitrary brain developed something out of paper that I guess, despite the industrial revolution, the space age, and the cyber explosion, will be a part of ours and every culture until the Lord returns.

Think about it. You start with a round number of fifty-two cards. Then you have, for no apparent reason, two cards with, of all things, a skinny person with bizarre clothing called a joker. These two cards are in here for no other apparent reason than, before use, to remove them.

This doesn't usually work out too well, and someone we refer to as the card police says, "Did you remember to take out the jokers?" which is merely a rhetorical question followed by sorting through all the cards to find where they are shuffled in.

If we're thinking the number fifty-two is random, the deck gets far better, composed of a system only the federal government could have thought up. As anyone who has successfully passed through the birth canal knows, there are four suits of cards, and none of these come with a tie and vest. Suits in this case means everyday items which are named one thing but look totally like something else. There are, logically, thirteen of each, and they are the following:

1. *A spade.* A small garden tool which looks good hanging in the garage but which is never used except in

commercials of cheerful women in work gloves and pretty straw hats advertising regularity medications. As you can well understand, this is the trump card. To reiterate, none of the suits look like either a suit or their name, so this is described as the upside-down black heart on a stick.

2. *A club.* A thing that you pay twenty-five dollars every January so you can either put that you are a member on your resume or get in a store that sells bulk paper towels for the same exact price per unit of regular paper towels but are harder to fit in your trunk. Also, a club is a thing that Fred Flintstone and Barney Rubble carry around to look posh.

    Clubs are beautifully portrayed on playing cards as a black stick with three circles on it. This is why some people call them clover instead of clubs because they are exactly like four leaf clovers, only they do not have four leaves, or leaves at all, and they are not green, and in the games I have played they do not bring good luck. This explains why people call them puppy dog feet. This is because some people are on heavy medication.

3. *A heart.* The most sensible of the suits because they actually do look exactly like red valentine-type hearts which look nothing, of course, like real human hearts which look like waterlogged pretzels.

4. *A diamond.* If your fiancé gives you a diamond which looks like this, and you accept such a gift, see a marriage counselor immediately. But see a regular counselor first.

Now it's important to know that each suit of cards is numbered, A through ten. That makes thirteen. This is because there are queens and kings and such. These are known as a royal flush. This is a good thing, especially to the lady in the work gloves and straw hat.

In most card games, the higher the number next to the upside-down heart on a stick, the more advantageous this is to your standing, so that if you have a ten, the only thing better than that could be a face card, and the only thing better than a face card could be a one. See?

There are no ones really, but there are A's which are, of course, much like ones. It may come as a surprise that the kings are ranked higher than the queens. It may be an even bigger surprise that there is someone in the royal palace named Jack. You have your queen, you have your king, and then there's Jack. No one knows who Jack is, but if you see him, slap him fast.

Through the ages, man has come up with a bazillion ways to play games with these fifty-two cards after you take the jokers out. Some of them also involve chips which you do not even eat, but put in your eye sockets and say, "Look! I'm little orphan Annie!"

Most variations of any of these games consist of taking turns to throw cards down on the table until someone randomly yells out a meaningful word such as "Nertz!"; "Woof!"; "Snap"; or violently grabs a spoon.

After centuries of this kind of organized play, you'd think the deck would be improved upon. You'd think there would be a more sophisticated way to keep up with the cards than a dry-rotted rubber band or a box with torn edges because it is easy to get them *out* of the box, but it's an irreversible operation.

This is why there are never quite fifty-two cards in my box, which is why most people I meet say that I am not playing with a full deck.

I think.

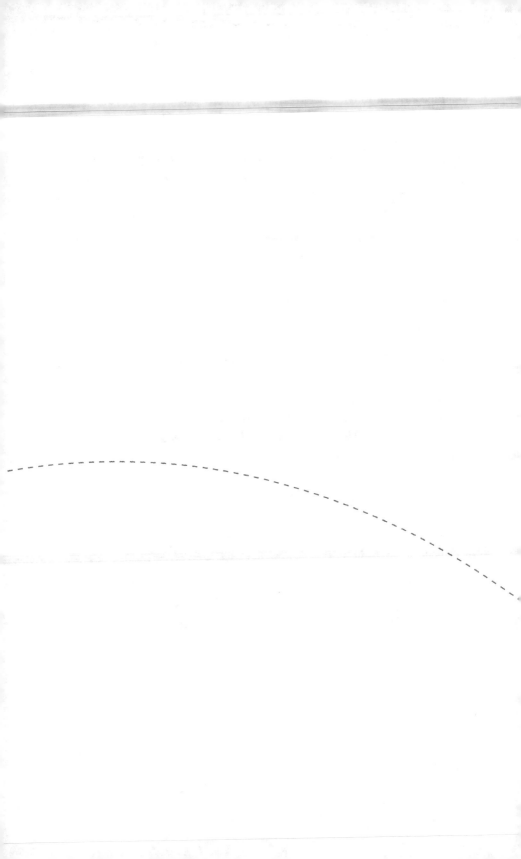

WORKS CITED

Barrie, J. M. *Peter Pan*. New York: Barnes & Noble Books, 2005.

Beaumont, Kathryn. "Your Mother and Mine." *Peter Pan*. Walt Disney, 1953, CD.

Brecheen, Carl and Paul Faulkner. *What Every Family Needs or Whatever Happened to Mom, Dad & the Kids?*. Austin: Sweet Publishing, 1979. Print.

Campbell, Kate. "Funeral Food." *Visions of Plenty*. Compass, 1998. CD.

Carr, Martha. *St. Augustine High School Students Rally in Support of Paddling*. Nola.com, 4 Mar. 2011. Web. 14 Jan 2014.

Cunningham, Ted and Gary Smalley. *As Long as We Both Shall Live: Experiencing the Marriage You've Always Wanted*. Ventura: Regal Books, 2009. Print.

"Desperate Housewives." yU-co, 2012. Web. 14 Jan. 2014.

Marshall, Christopher D. "Prison, Prisoners and the Bible." *Breaking Down the Walls Conference*, 14–16 June 2002, Matamata. Web. 15 Oct. 2011.

McCord, Hugo. "Sixty-Five Years as a Preacher." *The Spiritual Sword*, 26 Jan. 1995. Print.

Noyes, Betty. "Baby Mine." *Dumbo*. Walt Disney Records, 1941. CD.

"Old Woman Who Lived in a Shoe." Mother Goose Club. Sockeye Media, 2013. Web. 14 Jan. 2014.

Seuss, Dr. *Horton Hatches the Egg*. New York: Random House, 1940. Print.

Vos, J.G. *Genesis*. Pittsburgh: Crown & Covenant Publications, 2006. Print.

NOTES

NOTES

NOTES

NOTES